FVL

EARLY PRAISE F

SOULSHA

D040136З

"Spiritual erotica! Jeff Brown lays down his soul on these pages for us to see ourselves. In so doing, he demonstrates a rare vulnerability, a wicked sense of humor, and a deeply personal insight into the human condition." —KATHRYN BEET, master yoga practitioner and owner of Yoga Space, Toronto

"Jeff Brown takes readers on a journey seeking to find his inner self. It is a search for self-fulfillment, a field guide for life, and a quest for the meaning of life." —EDDIE GREENSPAN, QC, criminal lawyer and earnest defender of the presumption of innocence

"*Soulshaping* is a beautiful story of one man's spiritual journey that reveals the inspiring, yet often humbling, path of growth and self-transformation. Jeff Brown offers us a raw, honest, and humorous glimpse into the exploration of self, while also imploring us to celebrate the opening of the heart and the awakening of the soul—no matter where we are directed, what is revealed, or who shows up." —SEANE CORN, international yoga instructor and spiritual activist

"*Soulshaping* is lit with epiphanies and hard-won psychospiritual savvy not just for the author, but for all of us. Jeff Brown has faced his dragons and has emerged from the flames with significant treasures and a soul-centered, refreshingly raw travelogue that is as readable as it is instructive. A brave book this is—a book that serves our own journey of awakening and healing simply by being so unswervingly and nakedly human. —ROBERT AUGUSTUS MASTERS, PhD, author of *Meeting the Dragon*

"If you don't have a gut reaction to this book, you may be dead! My heart completely opened up as I felt each page come alive with emotion. It's a must-read for anyone on a spiritual path to identify and discover our powerful and majestic self." —JEWELS JOHNSON, host of *Law of Attraction Talk Radio*

"Tired of another by-the-numbers guide to spirituality? *Soulshaping* is the real deal, a gritty look at the reality of fully inhabiting your life. It may be the only soul-help book I have read that brings spirituality and psychology together in a grounded framework. I love the way Jeff Brown shows us how to shed our emotional debris and ego armor, while at the same time transforming all of it into the lessons we need. Nothing gets lost or misplaced—everything is grist for the soul mill! *Soulshaping* represents the next step in the spiritual transformation of Western culture, a perfect blend of Eastern mysticism and emotional healing. Brilliant and perfectly down to earth at the same time." —ZEYDL HEMREND, lawyer and film producer

"Jeff Brown takes us on an intimate, compelling, enlivening, and often quite humorous set of adventures with many of today's leading consciousness teachers on his journey to uncovering the deep truths that live at the heart of all spiritual paths." —ROBERT GASS, EdD, workshop leader, spiritual activist, composer, performer, and recording artist

"As a therapist and as a human being, I highly recommend *Soulshaping*. It is a must-read for anyone wanting to move beyond the profound emotional blocks of early wounding and gradually, very gradually, begin to awaken to increasing levels of self-acceptance through the wisdom and tenderness of their own essence. Through his school of 'heart knocks,' and with astonishing emotional authenticity, Jeff Brown implores us to embrace and fully 'excavate' our Shadow, the seeming darkness within. Only by fully honoring all aspects of our journey (every wound, every person, every trauma) can we begin to accept and eventually honor all of who we are." —JOHN POLLARD, MA, psychotherapist and spiritual director at Transformational Arts College

"*Soulshaping* was the most valuable, engaging, and hard to put down book I read this year. This book goes way beyond the rote 'how to' presented in so many spiritual books and offers a sincere and true-life story of what it is really like to journey into the inner world of self-creation and to listen, truly listen, to that tiny voice inside. Jeff Brown is the real deal and he shows with heartfelt honesty that there is no 'arrived' when it comes to the quest of the spirit." —DR. MELISSA WEST, international radio show host with Contact Talk Radio

"Just as a sculptor shapes his clay on the wheel, Jeff Brown shapes his soul from the wheel of his life. An alluring and riveting journey, a definitive cure for soul-dysplasia, this book is real! Never before have I read a book so eagerly anticipating the next page—not because of a mystery unfolding, but because I wanted to see if Brown had my story right. For those on their soul journeys, this book will no doubt reveal a different vantage point to help them find their way." —SUSIE BONHAM-CRAIG, spiritual psychologist and author and host of *Wisdom Wide Open Radio*

"If I were to use words to describe my innermost feeling after reading *Soulshaping*, I would use two: true inspiration. I believe this book will be used as a 'bible' to those who truly need a guide for their journey. Jeff Brown's life journey will truly inspire those who have started and then stopped, those who have a knowing, but don't know where to begin, those who have despised their life due to some traumatic experience at some point in time, and will realize by reading this book that they can go on!" —LAURA ANNICHARICO

SOULSHAPING

A JOURNEY OF SELF-CREATION

Jeff Brown

North Atlantic Books
Berkeley, California

Copyright © 2009 by Jeff Brown. All rights reserved. No portion of this book, except for brief review, may be reproduced, stored in a retrieval system, or transmitted in any form or by any means—electronic, mechanical, photocopying, recording, or otherwise—without the written permission of the publisher. For information contact North Atlantic Books.

Published by
North Atlantic Books
Berkeley, California

Cover art © Mattihappy/Dreamstime.com
Cover and book design by Susan Quasha
Printed in the United States of America

Author photos by Bibbles Ganoush
Permissions begin on page 181

Soulshaping: A Journey of Self-Creation is sponsored and published by the Society for the Study of Native Arts and Sciences (dba North Atlantic Books), an educational nonprofit based in Berkeley, California, that collaborates with partners to develop cross-cultural perspectives, nurture holistic views of art, science, the humanities, and healing, and seed personal and global transformation by publishing work on the relationship of body, spirit, and nature.

North Atlantic Books' publications are available through most bookstores. For further information, visit our website at www.northatlanticbooks.com or call 800-733-3000.

Library of Congress Cataloging-in-Publication Data

Brown, Jeff, 1962–
Soulshaping : a journey of self-creation / Jeff Brown.
p. cm.
Summary: "The story of a brilliant young trial lawyer who struggled to find his true path, this engaging, inspirational memoir takes readers through profoundly human terrain—unresolved emotional issues, economic obstacles, confusion, self-doubt, and what the author calls 'the school of heart knocks'—on a soul-searching journey toward heart-consciousness and spiritual authenticity"—Provided by publisher.
Includes bibliographical references.
ISBN 978-1-55643-810-3
1. Brown, Jeff, 1962– 2. Self-actualization (Psychology)—Case studies. 3. Spiritual life—Case studies. 4. Mind and body therapies—Case studies. 5. Spiritual biography. 6. Lawyers—Ontario—Biography. 7. Toronto (Ont.)—Biography. I. Title.
BF637.S4B814 2009
158.092—dc22
[B]
2009001905

7 8 9 10 11 VERSA 18 17 16 15
Printed on recycled paper

For Paul Hemrend
and the spirits of
Bernard and Frances Perlove

② July 2017

Contents

Gratitudes

Gratitude to those who encouraged me before I could encourage myself—my parents, Valentia Lee, Miriam Blumstock, Graham Northcott, David L. Mandel, Sharon E. Lavine, Rocketdog, Wendy Yamamoto, Judith (Leslie) Greenbaum, Nella Starai, Janice Nishimoto, Nicholas Brinckman, Sue Bennett, Arthur and Carol Back, Gloria Robbins, Ova Back (and her warm chocolate pudding), Joelle Glasroth, RJB, Dr. Ralph Kilmann, Esther Climans, Eileen Greene, Randy Richmond, Amy Baumal, Little Missy, Gary Schilling, Jackie and Shani Feldman, Dawn Stephenson, Lisbie Rae, Jill Goldblatt, Tony Melaragni, Fatima Lobo, Naomi Goldsmith, Louise Frechette, David (Skinny) Sniderman, Marta Cuellar, Janet L. Bomza, Amy Burke, Michele Spicer, Edmond Timmerman, Dr. Leo Shack, (Auntie) Judy Haid, Bibbles Ganoush, Dr. Tom Greening, John Pothiah, Avi Zimmerman, Abigail McClure, (Auntie) Mitzi O'keefe, Auntie Tilly, Martin and Stanley Resnick, and Uncles Ricky and Teddy Perlove. Thank you all from the bottom of my soul.

Gratitude to those lite-dimmers, double-crossers, space invaders, and plain old nasties who attempted, in word or deed, to force my light under a bushel. Your hurtfulness was grist for the soul mill, gifting me with the painful lessons I needed to learn. Without you to push against, I might never have found my way home. Glory to the school of heart knocks.

Gratitude to those bodysoul workers and healing places that supported my healing and expansion: Sandra Finkelman, Marika Pollak, Marilyn Morinis, Jim Bean and Beverly Yates, Dr. Christopher Hassel, Janice Greene, Rainah, Cora, Kathleen Mckay, Barb Towns (and her band of renown), Ruth Whalen, Laurie Ward, Lindsey Syred, Meenakshi, Esther Myers, Blake Carter, Katharine Beet (Yoga Space, Toronto), Angie Toccalino, Sarah Tomlinson, BarnCat, Downward Dog Yoga (Toronto), Jivamukti Yoga (Toronto), Rosa Laborde, Ramona Ng, the Kid, Redpaw Data Services, Yellow Brick Road, Deanna Villa, Diane Gordon, Clinic I Need, Barb Dewar, Suzuki Shiatsu, Anne Harris, Odette Schywiola, Jennifer and Chris Italiano and everyone at Live Health Cafe (Toronto), Christine Matheson, Fresh Restaurants (Toronto), Omega Institute (Rhinebeck, NY), Gibraltar

Point Centre for the Arts, Harbin Hot Springs, Samasati Nature Retreat, Saybrook Graduate School.

Gratitude to those soul blazers and champions who have touched and elevated my journey, reminding me of what I inherently knew all along: Rumi, Ram Dass, Alexander Lowen, Seane Corn, Coleman Barks, Robert Augustus Masters, Eddie Greenspan, Oprah Winfrey, Jean Houston, Jeanne Achterberg, Bhagavan Das, Anodea Judith, Sean and Robin Wright Penn, JFK, Kate Beckinsale and John Cusack (for *Serendipity*), David Wolfe, George Kaufman, Deva Premal and Miten, Amma, John Wayne, Natalie Portman, Penelope Cruz, Mary Oliver, John Pierrakos, Stan Lee, Nelson Mandela, Ron Kurtz, Krishna Das, *Rocky Balboa,* Drew Barrymore, Chantal Kreviazuk, James Hillman, Thomas Moore, Van Morrison, Abraham Maslow, *Seabiscuit,* Christopher Cross, Wayne Gretzky, Muhammad Ali, Terry Hunt, Forest Whitaker, Jessica Lange, Jack Kornfield, Stanislav Grof, Steve Carter, *Captain America,* James Taylor, Yvan Cournoyer, Guy Lafleur, Neem Karoli Baba, *Cinderella Man.*

Gratitude to dear friends and seeming strangers that helped to keep this book-writing expedition afloat by word or deed: Granny Franny, Elizabeth Lesser, General Scribbles, Michael Payer (Universal Glass Ltd.), Slim, Spicy, Jeffrey Abrams, the ever-beautiful and wise Tarini Bresgi, (Auntie) Corrine Wilks, Kathryn Bint, Glen Newbury, The Open Heart Gang, Maggie Zellner, Edna Khubyar, editors RonniLyn Pustil, Catherine Dees, and Diane Darling, Jean Christian, Sharon Sephton, Nancy Loucks-McSloy, Sylvia Ianeri, Alexander K. Rai, Tena Moore, Ken Preston, Tony Everest, Uncle Joe Perlove, Sophie Brown, the customers of Academic Glass Ltd., Kay Wong, Gilligan, Roberto Diamanti, Rachel Larabee, Faith Davis, Jongrok Choi, Jessica Weiser, Warren Sheffer, T. Wally, John and Jack A. Armstrong, M.J. Bogatin, Ethan Dann, Coach House Press, Monte Gagne, cousin Rocky Polson, Naomi Lir, Angela Spagnuolo, Yumee Chung, Sharon and Gordon Resnick, Pops Avalanche, Lela Iselin and family, Swaha, Jennifer Berezan, Wade Imrie Morissette, Wah, Lama Gyurme, Aeoliah, Snatam Kaur Khalsa, Zoey Shamai, Larry Back, Carmella Hatter, Joey Rappaport, that homeless woman on St. Clair Avenue who told me I had it in me when I looked downtrodden, Auntie Annie and Uncle Manny Perlove, Jerry Gladman, you.

Many thanks to Peter Beren and Mark Ouimet for supporting my work and landing me in the right hands. And profound gratitude to the lovely people at North Atlantic Books (Richard, Emily, Jon, Kathy, Susan, Sarah, et al.) and Random House for giving *Soulshaping* a larger set of wings and a better chance to fly.

Profound gratitude to my niece, Naomi Lir. So grateful that your warrior spirit overcame the obstacles and that you found your way back into my life. I honor your brilliance and your faith in this challenging but ultimately delicious human dance.

Hugs of gratitude to my spirit kid, Vanessa (Hot Tamale) Lees, for always reminding me that I am needed for what I bring. Your courageous insistence on living from your heart always brings me back to my own. May you love yourself, as Ragus loves you. Rave on, Tamale, rave on....

Boundless gratitude to Paul Hemrend, the greatest friend this soul could ever hope for, whose unwavering love and patience keeps my sails aloft on this often-hazardous ocean of meaning. Without your divine wisdom and support, *Soulshaping* might well have sunk to the bottom of that ocean, perhaps never to be seen again. Let's keep moving, Bauble. Let's keep shaping our souls.

Eternal gratitude to my grandparents, Bubbi and Beela Perlove. Bringers of the light, you stood beside me, in front of me, and within me every step of the way. I continue to inhale all the love you left behind. When I lose my way, I take a big breath of you, and the path becomes clear. You are forever woven into the seams of my soul.

Preface

I wrote *Soulshaping* over more than a six-year period, in the cramped and isolated back room of my house in Toronto, Canada. Written amid a tyranny of economic and personal challenges, I went back and forth between the back room and the marketplace, racing off to make a living, returning home to find the words. Although I longed to stop and breathe, the call to write was relentless, determined to have its way with me. If I spent too much time doing business, it mocked my materialism: "Enough! You met your basic needs. Now get back to the computer." If I went to bed too early, it woke me up in a start: "Get in the back room and write!" It soon became clear that honoring my calling was my only defense against sleeplessness. If I wrote, I slept. If not, I lay awake all night tormented by the words waiting, impatiently, at the gate of self-expression. It all seemed a little insane.

At the same time, I was riddled with shame and self-doubt. My calling was to write a subjective book, to talk about spirituality through the vehicle of my own journey. Yet every self-deprecating part of me rose to the surface to knock it down: "Who wants to read about your miserable journey. Why don't you keep these embarrassing experiences to yourself?" "You're not famous—who is going to buy your autobiography?" "This may serve some therapeutic purpose for you, but won't help anyone else." Nonetheless, I kept at it, both because writing it was helping my soul to expand, and because I had some odd faith that my story might actually help someone else. The little voice that knows.

I finished the manuscript in the spring of 2007 and sent it to a leading spiritual publisher. Soon thereafter, it was returned to me with a contractual offer to publish. My ego was elated—an offer, so fast!—but my spirit was deflated. Their editor had spent weeks chiseling away at it, cutting it virtually in half. It didn't look like my book anymore. Whose book is this anyway? Is this a blessing or a curse? Confused, I went away and compared our versions. At first, I was too attached to my voice to see the gift, as though it had been *my* voice that I was channeling (first mistake). But then my inner eye opened, and I saw the gift he had brought. My version was too long and repetitive, his leaner and crisper. I didn't agree with everything he did, but he gave me something that I didn't have when I wrote it—a reader's consciousness. Bless him, beautiful man.

But there was still a problem. My soul was grumbling. I didn't like the contract; something didn't feel right. It put a limit on the word count. I went inside and listened in. What did the little voice have to say? I heard the trumpets of guilt chastising me: "How can you turn down an offer after receiving such a wonderful gift?" Good point! I heard from my ever-practical ego, "You are exhausted. You are a first-time writer. You had an immediate offer. You fool—take it!" But I also heard a more benevolent, intuitive voice: "You have already opened the gift that the Universe sent you. Trust your intuition and bring this book into the world on your terms. Begin on the grass-roots level. You wrote with that intention, so honor it."

I refused the contract. I had written a book about the importance of honoring our soul-scriptures to the letter. How could I ignore mine?

I self-published (soul-published) the first edition of *Soulshaping* at the end of 2007.

I picked up a thousand books, and then wondered what to do next. Trust, Jeffrey, trust. I sold a few, then a few more, and then the emails started coming. They weren't just regular e-mails—they were emotional outpourings, cries of truth. Something about the self-revealing nature of *Soulshaping* invited readers to admit their own pain and their own longing for true-path. They said it was their story I had written. I was startled. Like many trauma survivors, I had grown up thinking that my family scene was different than everyone else's. When I was selling windows door to door as a student, I would knock on the door and then step back, somehow imagining that the world inside that home was somewhere above the world I had grown up in. As I read the response to *Soulshaping*, I realized that I was wrong. I was not the only one, not even close. So many of us have walked the same trauma trails and endured similar hardships. So many.

Then I encountered a bright-eyed homeless man who lived near my home in Toronto. I called him "the pushcart guru." We had an idea—he would sell the book on the streets. Seemed preposterous, until he sold a bunch almost overnight. And then people started to come looking for him. They would contact me—"I want to buy a book from the homeless guy!" The media came, we made a YouTube video, he sold dozens of books in no time. Then the Facebook group began to grow, people began quoting from the *Soulshaping* dictionary, readers sent in a bevy of book testimonials, and a free audio pod on my Web site—"the little voice that knows"—became so popular that we had to expand the site capacity.

Then the Universe kicked into gear, attracting people to the book under the oddest of circumstances—Serendipity galore. A friend called. She was with her friend in downtown Toronto when they formed the intention to go to the bookstore to look for a copy of *Soulshaping*. On the way there, they found one—sitting on a park bench. I had given a few copies away to a homeless man to sell the night before. He must have left one behind. Something was afoot.

My first press run almost completely sold out in a matter of months, without tremendous effort on my part, with virtually no bookstore coverage. Heartfelt gratitude to my soulpod. It takes a village to raise a book. Yet another bit of proof that we cannot achieve anything alone.

I went to sleep one night and had a vivid dream—I saw the book sitting on a bookstore shelf. The message was clear: This book was not mine anymore. It was for those who needed it. It was time to get it into the right hands. The Universe had spoken.

I contacted an agent I knew. He told me to call a particular distributor. By the time he returned my call, he had already recommended the book to three publishers, although he himself had never read it. With very little fanfare, a contract was worked out with North Atlantic Books for this edition. Their grass-roots philosophy is remarkably congruent with my own, and with the story of this little book. The little book with an energy all its own. When your mission is aligned with the Benevolent Universe, everything happens seamlessly.

This publishing journey has validated many of the things I wrote about in *Soulshaping*. First, it validates the faith I had in my inner voice—the little voice that knows. This voice carries a karmic blueprint for our destiny, whispering sweet somethings in our inner ear whenever we dare to walk a false path. Easily drowned out in this distracting world, it is the best friend we will ever have. Raising it to the rafters of consciousness is essential to our expansion. Second, the journey has confirmed the importance of gut-wrenching self-admission. So many of us hide our light under a bushel of shame, reluctant to show ourselves to the world for fear of being judged. But there can be no locked doors on the journey home. Admitting who we are is essential to our salvation. Everything has to be exposed. By exposing what lives inside of us, we liberate our own voice, and give others permission to self-reveal as well.

Next, the journey has reinforced my belief in unity consciousness. It is not just cliché—we really are all connected. Although many of the details are different, the essential threads of our humanity are remarkably similar: similar suffering, similar inner challenges, a shared longing for true-path. We are in this, together. We are *this*, together. Finally, it confirms that each of us is here with a profound purpose, however humble or simple it may appear. Growers are inchworms—real change takes time. But every little soul step we take is divine perspiration, shaping the individual and collective soul to the next stage of its evolution. I encourage you to do all that you can to overcome whatever obstacles you face on your path to truth. The path home is not always easy—the School of Heart Knocks is ever-challenging—but it is the only path worth taking. Your unique soul-scriptures live at the heart of you, lying in wait for their opportunity to be humanifest. They may be covered in dust, they may be hidden from view, but they are still there, still sparkling with infinite possibility. If my work can help to remind you, then it has served its purpose. I offer it with gratitude.

—Toronto, Canada
March 11, 2009

Beginnings

Who Am I, *Really?*

Some people pick up their tools,
Others become the making itself.

—RUMI

Through most of my early life, I felt connected to two seemingly different dimensions of experience. With the simplistic understanding of a child, I named them false-path and true-path.

In the early years, false-path was the most pressing—the outer life, the struggle for survival, my attachment to the identifications that kept me alive. Faced with a cruel home environment, I unconsciously adapted my personality to any path that offered relief. When I looked in the mirror, I saw the boy I had to be—the tough little fighter, the fast-talking distortionist. Like so many of us, I identified my personas as my self.

Now and then another image appeared. This image manifested itself erratically, in intermittent trickles and subtle tremors, but it had an odd sense of authority to it. Amid the intensity of my childhood, I could only hear its distant flute between battles, but I sensed that some part of me would eventually die if I did not create space for its emergence. I named this distant flute "true-path."

In university, the flute drew nearer. I heard it clearly one day as I caught myself spontaneously writing notes in the margins of my notebook: "You are not who you appear to be." Then, in the heart of an intense lovemaking experience, a little voice whispered in my inner ear: "*You* are not really here." I ignored it and carried on.

Then I heard it at the movie theatre while watching *The Untouchables*. When Al Capone told Elliot Ness, "You're just a lot of talk and a badge," it touched a chord of self-knowing. I repeated it to myself *ad nauseam:* "*You're* just a lot of talk and a badge." My first mantra.

Then the flute went quiet. In my efforts to overcome poverty, I fully adapted my inner world to the mantras of survivalism: "Never surrender! Never look back! Keep your nose to the grindstone!" With little getting through my armored shell, I fell out of touch with my inner truth.

As a law student, I would often go for long walks. As I walked, I looked with an inquiring eye at everyone who passed. If each person could find their way out of circumstances that hampered them—if they could get in touch with their deepest callings and live in harmony with spirit—how would they look? walk? act?

I became a Rembrandt of human potential, sketching an image in my mind of each person in his or her truest light. Although cocky (how could I know someone else's truth just by looking at them?), I was asking the right questions. I was just asking them about the wrong person.

After completing my law studies, my questions turned inward, inextricably linked to a fear of death. I began to avoid highways when I drove. I refused to fly. It wasn't really dying that scared me but the possibility that I would die while walking a false path. It seemed like the greatest tragedy to die while not really being there for it—to face my maker embodying a false consciousness.

One afternoon, while in line at the grocery store, I caught my own reflection in the mirror. At first, it didn't register that it was me I was looking at. I stared at the stranger and noticed his despair. When I recognized myself, I began to ask the right person the right questions: What would my face look like if I were living closer to Essence? Would my eyes be brighter? Would those lines around my eyes fade away? Would I stand more erect? Would I be more radiant?

One question began to dominate my inner landscape: *Who am I, really?*

I would touch a woman, and the question would arise: Who am I, really? I would plan a legal practice and there it was again: Who am I, really?

Even seemingly mundane experiences triggered it. Shopping for a courtroom suit: Who am I, really? Why are you choosing that suit?

Does it reflect your essential self, or someone else's idea of who you are? What would your essential self choose to wear?

At the heart of this inquiry was the quest for my *entelechy*. This word has stuck to me, and me to it, throughout most of my journey. Human Potentialist Jean Houston defines entelechy as "the dynamic purpose that drives us toward realizing our essential self, that gives us our higher destiny and the capacities and skills that our destiny needs for its unfolding." In the philosophy of Aristotle, *entelecheia* was the actualization of form—perfection, realization, fullness of being. Again in Dr. Houston's words: "It is the root self, the ground of one's being, and the seeded, coded essence in you which contains both the patterns and possibilities for your life."

In *Soulshaping*, the entelechy is understood as the pre-encoded being we came here to humanifest, and the tools we brought with us to humanifest it. It is the *real* who you are, the *real* why you are here. I will refer to it in many related forms—karmic code, innate image, and callings. Introduced by James Hillman in *The Soul's Code*, the *innate image* is essentially a tangible representation of the soulshape that we are here to embody.

Just before psychotherapist Virginia Satir died, she told Houston: "I have done what I came here to do." She had honored her entelechy. She was a rare being. Most of us do not recognize why we are here. Lost to the quest for material gain and ego strokes, we stumble from one misidentification to another, with no knowledge of the treasure that already lives within us.

I was determined to find it. On the verge of opening a legal practice, the quest for my entelechy overwhelmed me. As I moved toward a commitment to law, I was simultaneously pulled in the direction of … what? What I would later characterize as a blessing, I then experienced as a *spiritual "emergingcy"*—deeper calls rose up like irrepressible geysers, poking holes in my ego armor at will. The battle was on.

This book is primarily about the next stages of this journey. Although I was surely not ready to let go of my law career, I was just ready enough to postpone my commitment to it. When I did so, I anticipated a short period of clarification to be followed by a long career as a trial lawyer. Someone in the deep within had other ideas.

In writing this book, I have tried to stick closely to my subjective experience in all its intensity. This was the nature of the call itself, but it also reflects my own longings as I took the path less traveled. As I traversed difficult terrain, I longed for books that could take me deep into the heart of psychological and spiritual transformation. I didn't want the broad principles alone. I also wanted the nuts and bolts of daily transformation. I wanted to really *feel* someone else's experience.

Throughout the book, I have attempted to put words to the many voices that emerged along the way. The benefit of time allows me to convey them in articulate form, but they seldom came through this clearly at the time of the events. Most of the messages emerged in the form of hints and whispers, quiet sensations that beckoned me to walk one way or the other, and it was for me to interpret them in the heart of confusion. As I became more familiar with my inner terrain, I got better at it.

Although the chapters reflect the stages of my journey, there is some measure of artificiality to their construction. Transformational processes are seldom clean and crisp. Stages of the process overlap and interweave all the time, and issues that you may have attended to early come back to bite you long after that "chapter" is seemingly over. And, of course, each of us goes through the stages in our own order. I began with the psychological and moved steadily toward God. You may feel God with you from the beginning.

The Inner Treasure Hunt

I have come to honor the sacredness and beauty of the inner journey. Although Western culture is obsessed with the outer journey—substitute gratifications, material goals, Let's Go, Europe—it is actually the inner travelogue that needs our attention. Great achievements that await us in the outer world are nothing compared with the glory of inner transformation. It is our capacity to overcome our inner obstacles—the emotional baggage that blocks the path, the quicksands of shame and fear—that determines the course of our world. This is where the juice of life really is.

It is often difficult to find our way inside. There are many signs attempting to get our attention—illness, disenchantment with our games, hints and whispers of something deeper—but they are often buried below the distractions and worries of the day. In a chaotic outer world, the cries of the inner world can seem frivolous and unreal.

The mystic poet Rumi said that "there is an inner wakefulness that directs the dream and that will eventually startle us back to the truth of who we are." Optimistic, but is this necessarily true?

How many people do you know who have been startled back to the truth of who they really are? Probably very few, though we all know people who have chosen full-on unconsciousness, whose lives tell the tale. False-self prison houses a great many inmates.

To wake up, we must get off the wheel of outer ambition and set our inner alarm to truth. If we don't, we risk sleeping through the whole thing. But let's not pretend that it will be a comfortable sleep. The soul doesn't like to be set aside, and it will manifest its frustration in the form of grumbles and stumbles, fitful sleeps and pleasureless unions, until we wake up to the truth of our lives.

Waking up is hard to do. Although many Westerners do not actually have to worry about basic needs, the collective unconscious is still gripping at the root. Many of us are more concerned with barricading ourselves against assaults than surrendering ourselves to our deepest being. Focused on the imagined legions of doom at our doorstep, we become anything we have to become in order to survive.

To make matters worse, the culture is a minefield of distraction. Over-stimulated at every turn, we find that our ideas of the good life often organize around fruitless gratifications and (in)convenient fictions fed to us by corporate dream weavers, preying on the uncentered consumer to further their own ends. Hooked in and worn down, we fall dead asleep on the bed of the marketplace, unknowingly inviting it to creep into our dreamscapes and organize our thinking. There are enemies of the sacred everywhere.

Of course, the outer influences are only the tip of the soulberg. We wouldn't be so easily manipulated by the marketplace if we were at peace with ourselves inside. We worry so much about our future only because we are living in the pain of the past. *If you have one foot in the past and one foot in the future, you are pissing on the present.*

Overwhelmed and misidentified, many of us feel like we are imprisoned in someone else's skin. If we can look in the mirror at all, we are often left staring at someone we don't know. Our outer manifestation does not reflect our inner truth. Who is that masked man staring at me in the rear view mirror? Why can't I look at him for more than a few seconds before turning away? What are his eyes trying to tell me?

We often identify ourselves as the adaptations and disguises that have helped us to stay alive. I am accountant. I am nice person. I am lazy man. Our identifications feed us one limited version of who we are—that's your story, and it's *shticking* to you—but there are more authentic versions lingering below the habits of daily experience. To identify them, we need to make real efforts to distinguish our personality traits from the deeper archetypal currents of our lives. We need to be painstakingly honest about those patterns that support a soulful life and those that betray it.

Despite the challenges, we have to try. So many clamored and struggled to make it through the birth canal and died trying, yet we made it through. Why? So we could lie on the couch watching television? So we could wait for our deathbeds to finally wake up?

We made it through because we are needed here. We are each here to uncover and honor profound reasons for being. We are each here as part of the sacred dance, stepping on each other's toes and turning each other toward God, one clumsy step after another. Although the ultimate romance is with your own soul, it is our experiences together that give birth to the essential lessons. Every entelechy is a buried treasure, essential to the advancement of the collective soul. If we get off the dance floor, we postpone others' lessons too.

A homeless woman stopped me on the street one day and said, "We need your heart." I never saw her again, but her words echoed inside me for years and helped me find my way home. Whatever her circumstances, whatever her shame, she had a profound impact, at least on me. She was needed for what she brought. So are you.

We need to tell our own humble stories until the language of the inner world becomes part of our daily lexicon. You don't need to be a plane crash survivor or a famous person to have a story worth telling. Just look at the life you have lived—are there not heroic aspects already inherent in your life story? Is it not something that you made it here while others did not? Have you not already overcome an inner plane crash or two? And does not more heroism await you, if you choose to honor your innate image for this lifetime?

Although the journey home is often difficult, it is also wondrous. On the materialistic treasure hunt, satisfactions are fleeting. You get the thing, the satisfaction fades, and then you need some other thing. On the inner treasure hunt, your satisfaction builds. It's so beautiful to touch a new plateau of awareness, to view your self with a broadened lens, to shape your self with your own two hands. It is a magically creative process that gives you wings. Every time I unravel a piece of my karmic thread, I feel the God-self come a little bit closer.

What could be more beautiful than looking back at the end of your life and knowing that you did what you came here to do? Isn't this the way you want to close your eyes for the last time?

This book is for those determined to accept responsibility for how authentically they live and for the path that they craft with their own hands. To find your way, you will need courage. Lots of it. If you don't have it, fake it until you make it. Soulshapers are artists, but they are also warriors. It is no easy feat to shape the inner world. You need the heart of a lion to overcome the odds. *You need to fight for your right to the light.*

It is my hope that this book walks that fine line between respecting the uniqueness of your individual journey and speaking to that part of you that may need company as you set (and reset) your foot on the path. My story only provides a template, but there may well be themes that resonate for you. Perhaps knowing that someone went this way will invite you to walk a little bit further into your unique unknown.

As poet Mary Oliver's words suggest, courageously walking the path of *most* resistance is often the only chance we have:

One day you finally knew
what you had to do, and began,
though the voices around you
kept shouting
their bad advice—
though the whole house
began to tremble
and you felt the old tug
at your ankles.
"Mend my life!"
each voice cried.
But you didn't stop.
You knew what you had to do,
though the wind pried
with its stiff fingers
at the very foundations—
though their melancholy
was terrible.
It was already late
enough, and a wild night,
and the road full of fallen
branches and stones.
But little by little,
as you left their voices behind,
the stars began to burn
through the sheets of clouds,
and there was a new voice
which you slowly
recognized as your own,
that kept you company
as you strode deeper and deeper
into the world,

determined to do
the only thing you could do—
determined to save
the only life that you could save.

1 Adaptations and Disguises

*We get so much in the habit of wearing
disguises before others that we finally
appear disguised before ourselves.*

—FRANCOIS DE LA ROCHEFOUCAULD

As an infant, I had a very subtle and still inner narrative. I discoursed with my conception of God and quietly envisioned the breadth of the universe. But soon enough, I lost the tether to my subtle self. If I had kept my heart soft and open, it would have been eaten alive.

My soul came into this life in 1962, or about 36 years BC *(Before Consciousness)*. I was the first-born child of a Jewish mother and an Irish father living and warring in Toronto, Canada.

Dad had grown up under difficult circumstances, raised poor in the toughest part of town by his grandmother and two older siblings. He never met his father and had very little positive contact with his mother. Meeting my mother gave him a second chance at family, a new opportunity to establish structure and roots.

My mother grew up in a poor and overwhelmed Jewish family. At one point, eighteen of them shared a house. With no room to breathe, she found refuge in her fantasy world. Romance novels and crooners kept reality at bay. Marrying my handsome, Gentile father fed into her vision of being swept away to a fresh, new world.

Within three years, happily-ever-after had fallen on harsh times. Despite his profound intelligence, my father was unable to deal with economic reality responsibly. Evictions and bad checks fed my mother's poverty trauma. She verbally assaulted him constantly: "Get off the couch, lazy! Drive a cab! Be a man!" The insults drove him deeper into the darkness.

When I arrived their unhappiness spilled over the edges. With a new baby on the scene there was even less space to heal the past or clarify the present. My relationship with my parents reflected their own strained partnership. I became their mutual enemy, simultaneously a source of pressure and an outlet to release it.

A woman beyond the edge, my mother had closed her heart to stay alive. With so much pain locked inside, she needed a scapegoat more than she needed a son. When her fantasy life seemed unattainable, she explicitly blamed me: "It was better before you came along." She burnt me with matches when I experimented with fire. She shoved soap down my throat when I swore. She told anyone who would listen that I was bad. I grew up certain that she hated me.

My father had wanted a daughter, so I was already in trouble before I left the hospital. To the extent that my mother conveyed that I was worthless, my father pressured me to be perfect. Then, when I succeeded at something, he knocked me back down. Dad shifted back and forth between manic rages and menacing silences. He broke my baby finger when I was an infant and beat me many times.

When I was four, my mother lost my sister, Robin, after only a few days of life. Dad became more withdrawn and hostile, years later admitting that he wished I had died instead. Subsequently, my parents adopted my brother Stephen and my mother gave birth to my brother Daniel.

The conflicts worsened. Most weekends were spent fighting, trembling, screaming. When they weren't after me, my parents were attacking each other, fighting with neighbors, hating and hurting. We all lived at Deprivation Central, a family of love-starved narcissists clamoring to see our individual reflections in a tiny pool of validation. There truly was no rest for the wicked in the haunted house that was my family.

In the first sixteen years of my life, we moved nine times. My dad went bankrupt. One Christmas, debt collectors banged on the door with hammers in the night. As an adolescent, I basically stopped going to school. Battle-weary from home, I couldn't handle the attacks in the schoolyard. I became agoraphobic, hiding from a threatening world in the worst hiding place of all—an in-house battlefield. Better the devil you know.

A Shroud for Every Occasion

To cope, I covered over my essential self. I became expert at the art of pulling adaptations and disguises from a hat in the blink of an eye.

From an early age, I was a master shape-shifter. An "alter-boy" at the temple of distraction, I put much of my energy into finding inventive ways to avoid the moment. This *self-distractive behavior* prevented me from self-destructing in the heat of a too-painful reality.

My first disguise, *Hyperboy,* was always in motion, twitching and jumping, running and kicking. I jumped from project to project, room to room, determined to never sit still. Fast movement masked my inner world, shielding me from unbearable pain. I moved so that I wouldn't feel, and because a moving target is harder to fell. I was put on Ritalin to slow me down. It almost killed me. It slowed me down so much that I began to feel the horrors I sought to escape!

Encyclopedia Brown preferred to be a heady, detached observer of life rather than a participant. Repetitive thoughts and mind games kept the pain at bay. Many of my later struggles involved distinguishing an avoidant headiness from a soul-sourced thoughtfulness. Am I using my mind to avoid true-path, or to honor it? Are my brain waves moving me away from the ocean of wonder or deeper into it?

People called me *Badboy* because I was. I swore early and often. I lit fires when no one was looking. I hit little girls with garbage can lids. I was kicked out of Hebrew school and summer camp. I stuck "Kick Me" signs on the backs of people I didn't like. I abused others, as I had been abused.

Acting out dark emotions allowed me to move them out of their toxic holding chambers and helped to mask my fundamental terror. A child living in a war zone, I could stay out of touch with my own brokenness if I appeared nasty to my peers. The mask of the nasty boy fit tightly for many years.

The *Warrior* was my most significant adaptation and disguise. He protected me from injustice. Throughout childhood, I fought back against my parents' tyranny with great resolve. My mouth became my shield and weapon, and I fought for my rights with mouthpiece a-blazin'!

By the time I was eight, I had well-developed capacities for subterfuge, espionage, attack, and counter-attack. Of course, fighting back made matters worse. Where my brothers benefited by going quiet—children are wrongly rewarded for containment—my big mouth drew negative attention to myself. Yet, I had no choice. I would cajole myself to shut up, but the call to arms would not be silenced. I couldn't stand the sensations of defeat, nor the theft of my personal integrity.

In adolescence I became a defender of other people's liberty. When I wasn't an abuser, I was the protector of the schoolyard, verbally protecting the weak and unrepresented in a kangaroo court that I alone presided over. At summer camp I fought against petty tyrannies on behalf of others. Many camp counselors paid the price for their unjust actions with Tabasco sauce in their water glass. I collected superhero comics and imagined myself a member of the Justice League. Determined to bring justice to this dark world, I actually called this part of myself *Captain America*.

To this point in my life, I was certain that I was living someone else's life. This couldn't actually be my *real* family. This wasn't really *me*. It was all false-path. My real life was waiting down the road, somewhere over a mountain. I just had to stay alive until I found it.

First Signs

It was then that I turned on the television and saw Eddie Greenspan, a criminal defense lawyer in Canada. Eddie became very famous in the 1970s, winning many high-profile murder trials and strongly advancing the presumption of innocence. He had a clear vision of the injustices that few cared to see, and he made it his raison d'être to open eyes and effect real change.

From the moment I heard Eddie speak, he felt remarkably familiar to me. I had no words for it then, but I sensed that it was something beyond our shared Jewish lineage or devotion to justice. Through watching him, I began longing to be a trial lawyer in this lifetime. It didn't seem like an ambition so much as a *knowing*. Sometimes I would get strange flashes of the two of us working together in a courtroom.

As I observed Eddie, questions arose: Could my warrior nature be something more than a survival mechanism? Is there some deeper knowing in the heart of this chaos? Might the "accident" of my family have in fact been no accident? Did I actually choose this madness?

Most of the time I denied their significance—who has time for such imaginings in the heart of daily struggle? But sometimes I wondered if true-path was rising up to meet me.

If Eddie brought a breath of inspiration into my dismal days, there was more right around the corner. Just before I turned eighteen, my mother announced that she was leaving my father. When my whole family moved away from him, hope awakened in me.

Around the same time, I met a girl at school and we fell in love. Finally feeling like I had something to live for, I started delivering pizza to make money and began to do school work with an eye to university.

Over the next two years good things happened. I graduated with an 80% average in my final year of high school. I fell in love again. I got into university in another town. I made the dean's list in my first year.

The college years offered little respite from the family drama. My father came by when he needed money to survive. I gave it to him out of my student grants and ran out of money in the second semester. Back at my mother's apartment, the isolation and poverty was driving her crazy. She was beating my brothers with a broom. The apartment had punch holes in many of the doors, broken windows and ripped screens, plates of months-old food everywhere. I was in the middle of this, even from forty miles away.

On weekends, Mom locked herself in her room with the furniture against the door and sang eerie suicide guilt songs. When I came home to borrow the car for work, she assured me she would be dead before the last pizza was delivered. She took the phone off the hook, causing me to anxiously race back between deliveries to see if she was still alive. She attempted suicide during my second year of university. The war had grown deathly.

Plato's Myth of Er

Er was a soldier, slain in battle, who returned to life telling the story of what he had seen in the other world. He said that after his soul left his body, he went on a journey to a mysterious place with two openings in the earth, and two openings in the heaven above. In between there were judges, commanding those souls that they deemed just to ascend by the heavenly way, and those deemed unjust to descend into the earth. While these souls were departing, other souls were returning, some ascending out of the earth dusty and worn with travel, some descending out of heaven clean and bright. They seemed to have come from a long journey, and they went forth with gladness into the meadow, where they encamped as at a festival.

Days later, the souls went before a prophet who told them that they were to choose the life that would be theirs in the coming incarnation. Their choice was entirely their own responsibility: "The responsibility is with the chooser. God is justified." They were also to choose their own "genius" to be the guardian of their lives and the fulfiller of their choice. Then the interpreter placed the sample of lives to choose from on the ground before them. There were lives of every animal, and man in every possible condition: wealthy, poor, tyrannical, famous, diseased, healthy.

There was an interesting pattern in the selection. Those who came down from heaven, having "never been schooled by trial," often picked an evil life. Those who came up from earth, "having themselves suffered and seen others suffer," often exchanged an evil destiny for a good one. Once all the souls had made their choice, they went before Lachesis, one of the three Fates, and she allotted to each its chosen genius. Then the souls marched to the plain of Forgetfulness. That evening they camped by the River of Unmindfulness, where each soul was compelled to drink of the river water.

As each soul drank, all was forgotten. Then in the middle of the night there was an earthquake and a thunderstorm and they were all driven upward to their births, like shooting stars.

Birth of a Persona

In the heart of my family madness, the Huckster was born. With no one to help me fund my future, I needed an ally who packed a punch. Out of the (black and) blue came the aggressive voice of an enterprising and charming hustler.

I knew of someone who went house to house installing peepholes in the front doors. I bought a drill, and in the summer after first-year university, I began to work the subdivisions around Toronto. I marketed myself as the student alternative: "Student peephole specialist at starving student prices." I nagged. I persisted. I said anything to make a sale. It worked. I began to make a little money.

Soon I became hungry for more. Having lived under the canopy of unbearable poverty, any moment spent out from under it was delicious. I spotted another opportunity and began selling brass kick-plates and mailboxes in the subdivisions.

The shroud of the Huckster became the face that I showed the world. I hustled when I sold, hustled my professors for higher grades, and hustled my girlfriend with no remorse. Because the Huckster offered me relief from my chronic security issues, he had an open invitation to take my personality and shape it in his image.

As my journey unfolded, this persona proved to be a two-edged sword. The Huckster helped me to meet my economic needs, but he also kept me neurotically attached to money and the illusion of security. In later efforts to honor my callings, I had to struggle to distinguish his benefits from his costs.

Somewhere between hustles, I was also a perplexed university student, inwardly confused about career path. Although my conscious intention was law school, my undergraduate studies awakened other voices. I was particularly pulled to humanistic psychology. Like Eddie Greenspan before, I felt deeply connected to Abraham Maslow. When I read him, I lit up deep inside, like a homecoming after years at war.

One summer afternoon, I sat on a cottage porch, engrossed by Edward Hoffman's biography of Maslow, *The Right to be Human*. As I read, I felt a strong pull toward graduate work in psychology. My breathing relaxed and I felt clear and present, like I had again tapped into the well that held my deepest truth and callings. Could a soul be called in entirely different directions?

A few moments later, I bolted from the chair in a panic. I cleared all my clothes out of the rental cottage, jumped into my car, and raced back to the city long before the end of the cottage rental. As I drove, I heard the voices of pragmatism pounding inside my mind: *This world is all about survival. Psychology is about why things happen. If you want to build a life, live in the reality of what is happening. Realists have a chance. You are a first-born Jew from a poor family. You need to make money. Law is your path. You will be a great success in the courtroom.*

Forget that another call had bubbled to the surface, the Warrior sped me back to my driven life. The language of my journal writing at the time reflected his dominance, with repeated references to "being strong," "maximizing all," and "overcoming, overcoming.... " It was the language of a boy on a mission.

Fueling the warrior fire was an experience from the previous winter. A friend and I had stayed awake all night and then gone skiing in the morning. Hungry, we drove to a mall to get some lunch. When I got out of the car in the parking lot, Eddie Greenspan entered my consciousness. I had the strangest sense that I was about to encounter him. Silliness!

Then I walked into the mall and saw Eddie talking on the pay phone. Holy shit! How to make sense of this? Synchronicity? Universal Intentionality? No, no, it must be coincidence! But how did I know? Too crazy!

Over the coming months, I returned time and again to the odd sense that my path would have to wind its way through Eddie Greenspan, wherever it was headed. Soon thereafter I was admitted to law school.

2 Calls from the Inner Wild

None of us will ever accomplish anything
excellent or commanding except when he listens
to this whisper which is heard by him alone.

—Ralph Waldo Emerson

In a culture that prioritizes the ego above all else, we elevate adaptation at the expense of authenticity. Below our daily shticks are soul-quakes eager to erupt, but we reside too far from our essential home to notice the cracks in our foundation. Without attunement, the cracks often come through in insidious and ultimately devastating ways.

As Marc Gafni wrote in *Soul Prints:* "If we do not pursue our particular call, then the ghost of that call will pursue us, like a haunting that stains our days."

Consider the following as possible symptoms of your spiritual homelessness: chronic illness; listlessness; unconscious consumerism; self-distractive behavior; egocentricity and narcissism; nightmares; images of gloom and doom during waking hours; dullness of eyes; perpetual dissatisfaction; addictive behaviors; heartlessness; hopelessness; chronic rigidity; inexplicable agitation, rage, or grief. False path, soul's wrath?

The Distant Flute

My first year in law school was terribly uncomfortable. I was attending the most prestigious law school in Canada, and my self-concept didn't measure up. I nervously waited for the admissions department to send me back to where I came from: Who you fooling, Badboy? Law school? Presumption of innocence? As if! Presumption of guilt for you!

Intensifying my discomfort was a destructive love relationship that I couldn't shake. Susan made me so weak in the knees that I couldn't keep my hands off her despite her lies, thefts, and betrayals. She was addicted to crisis, and I hooked right in. When I wisely ended the relationship, I would be triggered back into it by my own abandonment issues. Fractured by a distancing mother, I couldn't bear to be left, even if I did the leaving. Crazy-making!

At the end of the school year, I sensed the presence of an inner knowing calling out to me. What I would later identify as my *inner daimon* first came through like a distant flute, beckoning me in the direction of another path.

Historically, the inner daimon has also been referred to as our genius, guiding angel, deity, higher self, and white shadow. The quarterback on the field of Essence, it carries our callings until we are ready for the handoff. Jung had a name for his—Philemon—and Socrates had one that said "no" when he was about to do the wrong thing.

The Warrior within me named my daimon *Little Missy*. This was not intended as a compliment. For the chauvinistic warrior, anyone named Little Missy was a demure lightweight that needed doors opened for her. It was a "man's world," after all. Whenever she appeared, he immediately attacked her. The interplay between the two would live at the heart of my journey.

During summer break the tensions in my relationship with Susan intensified. Tired and desperate, I went to Montreal for a week. One night I had a vivid nightmare. I was approaching a closed door when I heard a man's voice: "Don't go in there. Susan is in bed with Marcos. Don't go in there." Marcos was a waiter at the restaurant where she worked. I opened the door and found them naked on the bed.

I woke up sweating and reached for the phone. I called Susan, but there was no answer. I called Marcos's house and she answered the phone. The dream was literally true. Mortified, I hung up and drove home at breakneck speed. The abandonment trigger was excruciatingly painful, and I had to get her back to turn it off!

I found her at my apartment. We argued all day and I forgave her. This latest act of betrayal took things to a new level of contempt. I hated her, but more deeply, I hated myself. I hated my attachment to disaster.

It was then that I had a very different kind of dream. A small woman sat down beside me on the bed and stroked my head. She told me that I had worth. She said that I had been pushing too hard for too long. There were things I needed to attend to now, or I would not be able to move forward. She said I needed to take a break from law school and begin the work of healing my past.

I woke up with the intention of organizing a sabbatical from law school. But before the first call could be made, the Warrior convinced me that a deferral was a cop-out. Little Missy rose up, and these two commenced their first conscious negotiation over my soul's path.

At this time there was a marked imbalance. Warrior was assertive, Little Missy hesitant. But she adeptly argued that it would be better for my legal career if I took "just a little" time to lick my wounds. It was plain to see that I was not going to champion anything in my emotionally fragmented condition, so the Warrior acquiesced in exchange for a promise that I would return to the Justice League fighting fit and ready to rock. Promise made, I took a leave of absence.

That autumn the craziness with Susan continued to escalate until one day we crossed the line. How crazy does it have to become before we face our demons? We were driving on the highway, fiercely arguing about her disloyalty, when she opened the car door and tried to jump out. She had one leg already out the door before I could grab her firmly and bring the car to a stop. I pulled over and finally collapsed into tears. So oriented to survival, I hadn't cried in years. I wept and wept until I fell asleep in my car.

I called a therapist that day and then avoided her return calls for a week. How do you feel into your suffering when you are completely identified with the armor that shields it?

One afternoon Susan hit me and stormed out of the house. As the door slammed, the phone rang. It was the therapist. Good sign. After one session I recognized enough of my own victim-hood to commit to a therapeutic process. The victim perspective would ultimately prove to be wrong-headed (and wrong-spirited!), but it was a key perspective at this stage of consciousness. You have to acknowledge yourself as a victim before you can recognize the karmic choices that you made to become one.

Lightening the Load

Over the next two years, I devoted myself to my own healing. This was my first opportunity to step out of survival mode and explore the contours of my inner world. At this stage, the question was surely not "Who are you, really?" but rather "What the hell is wrong with me?"

In therapy I slowly made contact with the wounded boy who hid below the man. At first I was moving so rapidly that I couldn't find him. It was all I could do to sit still for ninety seconds. I tried to distract my therapist, but she was smarter than me. She instructed me to relax and deepen my breath. She insisted on silence for long periods of time and encouraged me to do yoga. She pushed me into my first bodily experience of stillness, whether I liked it or not.

With her help I recognized that my self-distractive nature was not limited to hyperactivity. It was everywhere. A master of self-evasion, I hid from painful feelings and deeper truths behind a myriad of mirages. The closer I came to center, the more irrelevant the images that entered my mind. I thought of anything, everything, to escape the moment.

I also realized that I had deliberately chosen intense relationships in an effort to distract myself from the moment. Intensity was habitual, but it was also avoidant. Conflict and chaos are effective ways of evading the moment. If I wasn't in the moment, I couldn't be hurt.

Thankfully I had reached a point where it had become more painful to distract than to confront. In the beautiful words of poet Anaïs Nin: "And the day came when the risk to remain tight in a bud was more painful than the risk it took to blossom."

Ideally, the shedding of tired patterns would happen with fluidity and grace—a pupa shedding its old skin at just the right moment and expanding into a butterfly. But it doesn't seem to work this way for most of us. For whatever reason, we repeat the bad patterns until we are on the edge of ruin.

I began a regular practice of staring at my face in the mirror—*mirror therapy*. Though it seemed a little crazy, it actually felt therapeutic.

Feelings came up when I looked into my eyes that were otherwise hidden from view.

As I became more still, I began to edge beyond my localized lens into a more universal perception. One afternoon I fell into a deep sleep and dreamed of an intense lightning storm. In my dream, I crawled down a cliff and hid in a small cave to protect myself. From the cave entrance, I saw lightning hit a group of trees.

Moments later, I was woken up by a crash on the roof of the house. I went outside. The giant oak tree at the rear of the property had been hit by lightning and shattered. The road was blocked, the roof damaged, and cars smashed. If the inner and outer eye are not connected, how could I have dreamed this just before it happened?

Perhaps there really is information everywhere. One morning, I was awakened before dawn. A voice from the depths compelled me to write on my wall: *Excessive analysis perpetuates emotional paralysis.* In other words, stop using your mind to avoid your heart. This mantra became a dear friend to me on the journey ahead.

During my sabbatical, I was ill-prepared to touch the depths of my wounds and longings, though I did manage to lighten the load. Perhaps more than anything, I created new associations with the moment. Sometimes healing is more about creating the right conditions for growth than releasing old pain. Before I could deeply release, I needed to distance myself from the battlegrounds of early life and taste a gentler reality. After months without drama, I began to see new aspects of my personality emerging from below my armor.

Just before returning to law school, I heard Little Missy coaxing me to take a longer sabbatical. Her voice was quickly buried below an avalanche of dissent. Although I intuitively knew that I could not climb the highest peaks without releasing more baggage, the call to law took precedence. Spiritual teacher Ram Dass often says, "You have to become something before you can become nothing," and so it was. I had a claim to stake and essential lessons to learn in the courtroom before this soul could unfold into nothingness.

Glimmers of Knowing

I went back to law school raring to fight the good fight. My academic performance this year was crucial to my career plans because in the summer after second year, students interview for articling jobs. Articling is a mandatory one-year apprenticeship that begins after law school ends. My grades in first year were average, and I needed dramatic improvement. Although my poor self-concept asserted that I would not attract good law firms, something deep inside drove me to excel. I finished the school year with three A's and the prize in Law and Medicine.

One of the courses was "The Practice of Criminal Law," a weekly seminar taught by Eddie Greenspan and his brother. Midway through the year, I encountered Eddie in the parking lot before class. When he began to talk at length about criminal law, I experienced an extended *déjà vu*. I remembered this moment, the words, the atmosphere, all of it, from another time or place. Had we had this conversation before?

At the same time, I heard the call to practice criminal law loud and clear. Where was this call coming from? If it originated in the persecuted circumstances of my childhood, how to explain these esoteric glimmers of "knowing" around Eddie? Had I actually stumbled upon an essential path that meandered back in time?

I was offered a wave of articling interviews, including one with Eddie's partner. During that interview I got the distinct sense that I was not a candidate for the one articling position available. Disappointed, I let it go. By Thursday I had offers from two other criminal lawyers. I promised to make a decision by noon. About ten minutes to noon, the phone rang. It was Eddie's secretary: "We want you in for a second interview."

I was led from the waiting room into a large office with a giant desk. Eddie walked into the office, looked at me, and said, "Oh, it's you."

I responded, "Oh, it's you."

Weird. I felt like we already had this interview, some other time, some other place. He told me that he never interviews the students anymore, but plans had gone awry and it felt like something he should do. He asked me why he should hire me. I answered, "Because I am just like you. I'm hungry. I come from nothing. I worked like an animal to get here. I understand the way you look at the world. We're from the same world."

He sat quietly for a few minutes, then said he would call later in the day. He did, and he hired me. Those parts of me tied to my poor self-concept were stunned, though a quieter voice told me it had been inevitable.

My final year of law school was easy. Secure in the knowledge that I had my dream apprenticeship to look forward to, the Warrior took a break. I soon became attached to the French word *accidie,* which I understood as one's intrinsic awareness of their unactualized destiny. Like a song you can't stop humming, it nagged at me for months. My sense that I was not who I appeared to be was intensifying.

Although I didn't realize it then, another calling was beginning to insist on a seat at the table. Little Missy had a method to her madness and picked her spots with wisdom and care. Like a pied piper of Essence, she knew which street to walk down, and when, to gather her following.

One aspect of my calling that found its way through was the desire to heal people through my love of psychology. With no chance of ruling my consciousness just yet, it emerged from hidden chambers with an offer of partnership for the Warrior. I spent much of the school year imagining ways to humanize the courtroom.

The sound of the distant flute also emerged in my business life. On the drive to work on Saturday mornings, the flute would inch very close. As I pumped myself up to sell windows, I would be overcome by feelings of dread and sadness. Sometimes I had to pull over to the side of the highway to gather myself. If there had been words to accompany the feeling, they would have been these: "Stop wasting your time living someone else's life. Your daily activities do not reflect who you really are! You can survive by being true to yourself. What happens if your mask gets so thick that you can't take it off?"

The flutist was wise. She knew that the pulls of the culture are strong and that I could easily get routed to the wrong flight path. It is especially easy to get lost when you don't know where your real home is and when you're not quite ready to look for it. These little reminders, annoying as they can be in the moment, actually keep us from straying too far from true-path. They are blessings in disguise.

To appease Little Missy, I would sit in my car, or stand in a portable washroom in the heart of a new subdivision, and spend a prayerful moment saying farewell to my essential self: *"Soulself, I will be back, and one day I will not live so far from you."* Then I breathed deeply, put on my sales mask, and assertively door-knocked to make money.

At this time, it did not seem possible to live outwardly in ways that were in harmony with my inner voice. Either I lived in my false self and in the world, or I lived authentically, inward and detached.

A Blast from the Past

Soon after law school ended I began my apprenticeship with Eddie. I was eager to work like a dog, although oddly I had no interest in a hire-back. The drive was emanating from some other part of me, hidden from view but powerful in influence. Sometimes the essential self speaks in clear language, and other times it motivates in silence, quietly lighting a fire within.

When I opened Eddie's trial list for the year to come, there was a name that looked strangely familiar. Had I read this trial list before? Eddie handed me trial documents to prepare for him. After a few hours, little spikes of energy began to move through me. It felt so familiar. I stayed up all night crafting a defense. Something inside told me that I had prepared trials before.

Eddie and I worked an inquiry together a few weeks later. It all felt inevitable, like I was watching a re-run of a favorite old film. When it ended, he told me that I would junior for him on his biggest case of the year, a highly politicized murder trial. The accused was the same one I had recognized on the trial list.

I worked tirelessly helping to prepare the murder trial. The prosecution had crafted a case rich in forensic subtlety, and I was challenged at every turn. Under enormous pressure, I unearthed knowings that startled me time and again. It wasn't just a question of basic ability or gifts. It was a matter of experience. I approached the task like a long-established trial lawyer. There was no doubt: this hard-working student was no student in fact.

When the trial began, I stepped deeper into my experience. There was a trial warrior living inside me, and he was happy to be unleashed. Unusually comfortable in my own skin, I felt an ease in the court that one feels in their own home. I had been here before.

The nature of the work was no less familiar. I wrote elaborate cross-examinations. I helped to deconstruct the prosecutor's case and craft a defense far broader in scope. At the end of the trial, I wrote most of the first draft of Eddie's lengthy jury address in four days and nights, the pages coming out of me as though pre-written. This was not my first jury address.

Most familiar was Eddie himself. What I had first sensed watching him on television was confirmed by the reality of daily contact. I implicitly understood his perception of justice and the vision that sourced it from an essential place within me. Oftentimes, I would seem to know what he was going to say to a witness before it came out of his mouth. These moments confirmed that I was apprenticing with a member of my essential family.

I also experienced many *déjà vu* moments with him. I would be observing him at trial and I was sure that I had experienced that exact moment before. It was as if I were sitting back watching a film that I had already seen. As it happened more often, I began to wonder: What if *déjà vu* was the inevitable manifestation of a moment pre-encoded within me? Perhaps it was a sign that I was actualizing my *soul-scriptures* (the transcript of the innate image) exactly as written.

After the trial was won, Eddie asked me into his office. He asked me about my future plans: "How do you feel about criminal law? Where do you want to work?" I tried to answer him, but everything felt like a lie. My inner voice was whispering, *"This is the end of this dance."* I gave him some trite answer and left his office.

I went for a long walk to think it through. As I walked, I momentarily glimpsed another story breathing inside me. It was hazy but clear in one respect: the path of the trial lawyer was over for me. In it, I had worked like a dog with Eddie for only one reason: to quickly learn a lesson and move on.

By the time I got back to work, this story had faded completely from view. It was too early for me to read from that book.

I ended my year with Eddie at peace with path. The Warrior was delighted. Hyperboy was hyper-happy, certain that trial law would keep me mobilized and self-avoidant for years to come. And the Huckster was at peace because I wouldn't have to knock on other people's doors to survive—they would knock on my door now. I could finally satisfy my economic needs with dignity. Law was my imagined protection against the hounds of winter.

Most of all, my ego was satiated. I had been on television with Eddie. Supporters of the accused had given me a long ovation at a post-trial party and presented me with gifts. The judge reportedly told Eddie that the jury address was the best he had ever heard. Eddie paid for a two-week Caribbean vacation for me and my new girlfriend, Robin. I had known an extraordinary apprenticeship.

After a lifetime on the outside, I had a foothold in the world itself. No more chronic state of shame. No more standing-room-only. My ego was sitting in the gold seats. I walked around town like a king on the prowl. Oh, the power of the ego! On the cusp of entering into a lifetime of lawyering, I believed myself a happy Warrior: fearless, full of myself, eager to do battle with the tyrannies around us. Who dares to argue with a happy Warrior?

Bare Essentials

Then I heard it, loud and near. The distant flute, so quiet all year, began to play again. I went with a friend to Turkey for a last vacation before the bar admission course. Flying out of Istanbul to the coast, my bag was misplaced by the airline. I had only the clothes on my back.

The loss disoriented me. I couldn't sleep or soothe myself. So far from home, my clothes were my security blanket, the umbilical cord to wherever it is I came from. I felt especially vulnerable because I didn't really know the person below the blanket.

I bought what little was available—baggy Adidas shorts, tight-fitting Benetton T-shirts, nylon underwear. Initially I felt uncomfortable in my own skin. These silly clothes were not me! In search of something to calm myself, my mind wandered back to images of Canada. I had no template for the possibility that my real home lay within.

A few days later, a nagging voice whispered in my inner ear: "You have a choice. Stay open, stay open." Too lost in my defenses to appreciate its value, I resisted. Yet it persisted, encouraging me to try on a new way of being: "Your clothes are not you," said the voice. "Experience their absence as a gift. You will only know yourself when you are bare."

As I rode a bus through a foreign landscape, my inner lens suddenly opened. I began feeling strangely connected to someone more authentic living inside me. I could feel him there, close at heart. By the time we arrived at the small village of Kas, I had begun my first adventure in soulshaping.

Marcel Proust said that "the real voyage of discovery consists not in seeking new landscapes, but in having new eyes." For this brief moment, I understood. I wandered around the village feeling alive to its beauty. Unencumbered by familiarity, I had my first taste of unity consciousness. Rather than experiencing myself as separate from the village, I felt at one with it. I was not looking at the rough hills—I was the rough hills. I was enveloped in oneness.

One morning, I boarded a boat for a day cruise. As the boat sailed past islands, I lay on the deck listening to Enya's *Watermark* on my Walkman. Lying with my eyes closed, I looked inside and saw an eternal network of pathways. It all felt new and yet very, very old, and it made everything that came before seem small and tight and somehow unreal.

After lunch the captain announced that we were going to visit an ancient underwater village. As the boat came upon it, I could see the hill that stood above it. I sat straight up. My God, how familiar! My senses came alive. I *knew* that rugged hill. I saw warring tribes coming over the crest, coming down toward us. My heart raced. I stood up and looked down into the water. I saw the remnants of the village, *my* village. I had lived here, fought here, died here. My Western mind rose to protest: *Are you nuts?* My Western mind sat its ass back down. This experience spoke too clearly—I had been here before. I began to gently cry.

It was clear that my usual perception was only one reality among many, a singular framework of possibility fed by a narrow range of life experiences. I was on vacation, vacating the familiar, and up came the songs of prior selves, multiple selves, other worlds I had known. Crisp and clear, the music was unmistakable. What I had previously identified as Jeff was only a small part of the story. Below my timely concerns was a timeless self, bridged to deeper callings and eternal rhythms.

A few days later I flew to Santorini in Greece and rented a cave villa. My villa was seventy steps down from the village and carved into the face of a cliff. It was too hot to climb back up and so I took to sitting on the terrace and writing in my diary. At first I couldn't find a voice that felt alive, or true. Perhaps so many years of writing obligatory essays had numbed me. But I stayed with it and slowly discovered a voice that was authentic. Floating the pen across the paper, I touched into the flow of a vast universe. Who I was here was limited only by the breadth of my imagination. By the end of the week, I had arrived at the clear sense that one of the reasons I was on this Earth in this lifetime was to write. The call was unmistakable. The flute was in my hand.

I flew home to North America baffled. I was coming home to finish the bar admission course and become a lawyer. What a great thing— to help people while claiming my stake in the world. But so many unsettling questions were turning in my head. I had touched into the call to write. What, then, was my call to the courtroom? A mirage? A shallow pull? An ego path? Was there one true calling, or were there many? Could I shape my path with my own intention, or was it already carved, simply awaiting detection?

Landing in North America momentarily grounded my confusion. I knew who I was here. I cleared customs and walked into the terminal. One of my previous traveling companions stood waiting for me. In her hands was the bag that I had lost in Istanbul. Huh? She said it had been handed to her at an Israeli airport. In Israel, you say? A bag lost on the tarmac in Turkey given to someone else in Israel and then returned to me in Canada right after my adventure ends? Feels real strange. Must be a coincidence. Yes, that's it, a *coincidence*.

I'm Having a Pre-Life Crisis!

In a foreign landscape, unencumbered by familiar places and ways, there had been space to explore my identity. But returning back to the practical world, I had little regard for the esoteric. If an experience wasn't useful, it got put away.

Through this lens, the sense that I lived "in disguise" at home quickly transformed into the certainty that I had been out of my mind abroad. The searcher, the writer, the poly-phrenic soul faded from view. By the second week of the bar admission course, I was again the Warrior ready to take on the world.

I agreed with a group of peers to practice together after we passed the bar. We found a suitable office on a street of experienced trial lawyers. The rent was manageable. I was excited and confident. With career momentum and friends in high places, I had no doubt about my capacity to quickly build a thriving practice.

As the moment approached to sign the lease, my body recoiled. I felt like a powerhouse sprinter with his feet in the blocks, but frozen in time. I had intense nightmares around death and loss. The message was clear: *Stop! You must not sign on the dotted line!*

I decided to spend the Christmas holidays lying on my couch. Just to see. Just to listen. What is this voice in the night? A blessing in disguise, or a tricky saboteur?

As the days passed, I discerned two strands within me. The first was familiar: the Warrior, the Pragmatist, the Survivor. They pressed me to jump into the world: Seize the day! The other strand, vague but persistent, hinted at another path. For now, the details of that path were Little Missy's cross to bear. She nudged me to live in the mystery. What mystery?

> **Little Missy:** Come on. You need to explore the mystery. You are still too much the Warrior. You will be rewarded for your aggression by an imbalanced culture. Let it go or you'll never know why you're here.

> **Warrior:** I'm a man of action, and the courtroom is my true home. Law is my calling. I'm here to use the courtroom to fight injustice.

> **LM:** There is injustice everywhere. The greatest injustice is failing to do what brought you here this time around. Each person has a role to play. Law is not yours. If you do it, you take someone else's part and miss your moment. Sit still until the smoke clears.

> **W:** Look where I come from. My family is poor. Uncle Ricky died before he could actualize his abilities. My father is a brilliant man, immobilized by depression. My grandfather walks up and down the street telling people I worked for Eddie Greenspan. I worked like an animal to put myself through school. I slaved over a hot trial for months on end. Why? For this moment. To make THIS move!

> **LM:** The body wants shelter, the soul longs for meaning. Choose meaning. If you hook in now, you will get caught in the net and never get clear. Part of you knows that there are other worlds inside you, burgeoning with life. You need to extricate yourself from what you know best so that they can come to life. If you are a true warrior, you will postpone this decision. Dwell in possibility. Surrender.

> **W:** Never surrender.

My nights were fitful and angry, dark nights of the soul that left me sleepy and agitated. Images of possible futures rose and fell like arrows, stoking the fire of my confusion. I took to calling this state of being a *spiritual emergingcy*—the condition of confusion and inner tumult that one experiences when a spiritual path or awareness is forcing its way into consciousness, prior to its full emergence and integration. As some parts fight for new territory, others fight for that which they have already claimed, and you lie on a stretcher in the *emergingcy* ward in between, hoping that they all find a way to live harmoniously inside you.

I stumbled from one side of the battlefield to the other, a double agent by default. I was overwhelmed with endless questions: Will I find peace in law, or lull myself to sleep? Is law just a momentary visit with an old way of being? Is this the lifetime that I am supposed to cross over into new realms, or am I to push the soul envelope a little before returning back to the familiar? Where lies true-path?

At the same time, I was faced with another major decision. After tolerating my unwillingness to commit, Robin was all over me to put up or shut up. I was afraid to lose her, but how could I find *us* before finding myself? Was the law student she fell in love with the real *me,* or was *I* someone entirely different? If I didn't know who *I* was, how could I choose a life partner? *Who* does the choosing?

My mind kept returning to my Europe trip—the lost bag, the past lives, the call to write. In just a few weeks away from my usual routine, I had opened to an entirely different self-sense, a vaster universe of perception and memory. This experience gave me hope that there might be something worth searching for and a better way to get there—something courageous and expansive rather than safe and sound.

After a month I made the decision not to sign the office lease. I spent the rest of the winter in that agitated place between direction and exploration, experiencing neither the relief that comes with knowing where I am headed nor the joy of surrendering to the unknown. I would watch trials and leave frustrated because some other lawyer was stealing my thunder. I would walk toward Robin, eager to surrender to her loving embrace, and then sabotage it by running away. I wanted to bridge to deeper callings and clarify my path, but all I knew was confusion.

What now, Little Missy? Where to land? Where to stand? When do the calls from the wild civilize? Who am I, *really*?

There is one thing in this world that you must never forget to do. If you forget everything else and not this, there's nothing to worry about, but if you remember everything else and forget this, then you will have done nothing in your life.

It's as if a king has sent you to some country to do a task, and you perform a hundred other services, but not the one he sent you to do. So human beings come to this world to do particular work. That work is the purpose, and each is specific to the person. If you don't do it, it's as though a priceless Indian sword were used to slice rotten meat. It's a golden bowl being used to cook turnips, when one filing from the bowl could buy a hundred suitable pots. It's a knife of the finest tempering nailed into a wall to hang things on.

You say, "But look, I'm using the dagger. It's not lying idle." Do you hear how ludicrous that sounds? For a penny an iron nail could be bought to serve the purpose. You say, "But I spend my energies on lofty enterprises. I study jurisprudence and philosophy and logic and astronomy and medicine and all the rest." But consider why you do those things. They are all branches of yourself.

Remember the deep root of your being, the presence of your lord. Give your life to the one who already owns your breath and your moments. If you don't, you will be like the man who takes a precious dagger and hammers it into his kitchen wall for a peg to hold his dipper gourd. You'll be wasting valuable keenness and foolishly ignoring your dignity and your purpose.

—RUMI

24

3 Clearing the Debris

The only thing to do is to quite painfully unmask.

—CHÖGYAM TRUNGPA

The Mystery began with my history. As winter blossomed into spring, I sought an epiphany that would clarify my path in the safest place I knew—the courtroom. It was my sanctuary and the closest thing to home I had yet experienced. I picked up the pace of my visits to watch trials, sitting quietly in the back in anticipation, watching, waiting for an answer.

But something unexpected began to happen. Images of old suffering began to flood my courtroom visits—my mother's unhappy face, my father's backslaps, hiding under that stinky bed. With the images came the feelings, bringing me back to the memories of a childhood with no fixed address.

That spring, the first dam burst. As the Warrior sat focused at the back of the courtroom, tears poured out of his eyes and drenched his superhero mask at will. Sometimes I went to court after lunch and cried straight through until dinner.

For many months, the courtroom was the only place I could cry. Although this was initially puzzling to me, it made more sense later. Because of the insecure nature of my early life, I was frozen at the first chakra stage of emotional development. Called *muladhara* in Sanskrit, this stage relates to feeling grounded and safe here on Mother Earth. Now that I had qualified as a lawyer, I knew that I was no longer doomed to a life of poverty. Now it felt safe to let my sadness out.

As I released, the emotional memories grew more intense. I began to really *feel* my childhood experiences. I remembered how it felt when my father tried to strangle my mother. I remembered being angry and putting my hand through my bedroom window. I had no idea that I was still carrying so much old pain.

My inner world became like a series of beaver dams, each with more painful memories lying in wait behind it. Every time I cleared one away, another appeared. I felt a longing to completely fall apart, but my defenses were well entrenched.

Encyclopedia Brown jumped to the fore. I began to analyze my feelings to avoid feeling them. Whenever I felt the impulse to cry, I would find myself thinking through my suffering, as though thinking alone could actually heal me: What are the roots of my negativity? How did this suffering impact my development? Eventually, the feelings would fade. Mission accomplished—I was again a *numbskull.*

Beneath the numbness was a burgeoning movement toward authenticity, and clearing debris was essential to it. Anguish before beauty; worst things first. As it often would, the resolution of my inner conflict rested on the answers to two fundamental questions: How badly did I want an authentic life? What price was I willing to pay to create one?

Jabbed (Jealousy, Abandonment, and Betrayal Trigger)

As I surrendered to my pain, I began to identify some of the core issues that obstructed my path. The first to appear has proved to be the heaviest one to move. It was born in my difficult early relationship with my mother, and I took to calling it *JAB:* the Jealousy, Abandonment, and Betrayal trigger.

Up to this point, my intimate relationships with women had been mostly hostile and aloof. Modeled on my relationship with my mother, moments of closeness were inevitably followed with distancing. Like a warrior in enemy territory, I would sneak in and out of my girlfriends' lives in the night, plundering and taking what I needed, then crawling back to the other side of the abyss with the spoils. I gave little back for fear that I might appear interested.

Women fed into this way of relating with their own patterned responses. Rather than leaving me, as they ought to have, they looked on the bright side and believed that I was not the man I appeared to be. The truth is that I was exactly as I appeared to be. I was a bully and a user, with no template for intimacy.

Eventually women would grow tired of my games and leave me. Then I would enter a complete abandonment frenzy. JAB usually began with dizziness, cold sweats, and a gut-wrenching ache in the pit of my stomach. Then the nightmares and insomnia. I would enter an emotional abyss and forget all the legitimate reasons why the relationship was not a fit. All I wanted was my mommy back....

Next, I fought to get her back. I called her and wrote wordy letters describing how much I had changed—in only a week! I waited for her at work. Hope buffered me against the horrible pain of JAB. Without the dream of re-connection, I was lost to the horrifying sensations of a loveless childhood.

Often, a girlfriend would come back. For a few weeks it would feel wonderful. Then I would distance myself and the cycle would repeat. This impossible dance of isolation and fusion went on for years. I couldn't get close, I couldn't get away. No rest for the abandoned.

When we are ready to confront our issues, we seek them out. That autumn, I pulled far away from Robin. After months without contact, she hooked up with someone else. Stabbed by JAB, the proverbial knife twisted and turned in my belly day and night.

Typical of my pattern, I analyzed the relationship sixty times a day. I wrote Robin a sixteen-page letter promising to commit to her, marry her, make babies with her: "I love you more than words can say!" I did anything I could to build a bridge to her—all of it to avoid feeling the painful wounds that were uncovered without her. Grabby jabby.

Robin had her own lessons to learn. Eventually she granted me another chance. We went to Greece on a vacation. When we got home, I sabotaged the connection for the last time. She ran away, only this time I didn't chase her for very long. Something else was brewing.

A Frightened Little Kid

The call to change began as most transformations do—a subtle form with no discernable texture, a microscopic breeze that signals a change in wind direction, a little voice speaking in tongues—that we either trust without knowing why, or ignore at our own peril. In the middle of my terrible pain, some benevolent impulse was directing me: Feel your sadness, stop this madness!

Over the next few months, I trusted this impulse. Whenever my thoughts turned to long-winded letters and long-stemmed roses, I lay on my couch inviting the primal terror to rise to the surface. I was boldly going where this man had never gone before.

That winter I went alone to the Caribbean for a two-week vacation. In the first week it was all I could do to keep from flying home. I was still in the throes of the abandonment trigger, and the isolation made it worse. As I moved closer to the anguish, Badboy prodded me to go down to the pool to meet a woman. The Warrior instructed me to stop pondering my navel and be a man!

By week two, I was immobilized. I lay in fetal position in my hotel room for hours at a time, surrendering to excruciating waves of JAB. I needed to call JAB-busters, but they were nowhere to be found. I had no footing, no adult self, no friend strong enough to pull me out. It was just me, and me alone, plummeting through a primal abyss. Is this how I felt as a little boy? Poor soul—how did I survive?

After days alone in my hotel room, I began using what I call *depth charges,* actions taken with the intention of triggering unacknowledged issues and repressed emotions into awareness. Since most of my defenses were formed as a bulwark against unmanageable feelings, I needed to make intentional efforts to break through them if I wanted to feel my truth.

The first depth charge involved going to dinner for the purpose of consciously excavating my fear of others and noting my reactions. This was the perfect opportunity to do it because I was so raw and exposed.

I noticed that my hyperactive defenses took over even as I walked to dinner. I moved more quickly as others approached, and I avoided eye contact. At the busy restaurant, my breath became shallow. I spoke quickly to the waitress and ate rapidly. If I hadn't set the intention to pay close attention, all of this would have happened out of my awareness. How easy it is to know nothing about ourselves!

Next, I came back to my vulnerability by slowing down around others. I intentionally slowed my breathing and ate slowly. I stayed at the table for an unusually long time. As people passed, I noted my response to them.

At some point, the diners in the restaurant began to scare me. I wanted to race out of there. Slowing things down had excavated the frightened little boy that lived below my Hyperboy shtick. I was beginning to understand a fundamental principle of this process: any movement away from reactivity is a movement toward our truth. The next day I flew home.

I was now in a state of invitation, giving implicit permission to other memories and feelings to rise from the shadows and reveal themselves. There appeared to be no turning back. The onion was peeling itself.

That night, I lay on the floor in fetal position until I fell asleep. In the middle of the night, I awoke and wrote on the wall:

> Breathe into your frozen chambers,
> air trapped beneath blocks of icy blood;
> Loudly exhale the dust of lineage,
> dirt swept onto your skin
> by those who promised you gold,
> but gave you worms.
> God is buried within.
> Grab a noisy shovel, and dig yourself out.

After I finished writing, I went to the twenty-four-hour store and bought a tub of cheap butterscotch ice cream. I ate it in a desperate search for comfort. But there was no comfort to be found in butterscotch ice cream.

A Nervous Breakthrough

Over the next months, old pain rose feverishly to the surface of my life and deconstructed my usual ways of being. Trigger-unhappy, I fell completely apart.

At first I compared my state to a nervous breakdown, but this wasn't quite right. In a survivalist culture, breaking down is a sign of weakness. Yet this coming apart certainly didn't feel weak. In fact, it took all the courage I could muster to stay in it. I eventually recognized that I was having a *nervous breakthrough*—a profound emotional cleansing, a collapse of the false structures that had ruled my life, a breaking through to a more genuine state of consciousness. What seems like weakness to a survivalist is actually a sign of strength to a spiritual warrior who longs to be authentic at all costs.

I spent lots of time in front of the bathroom mirror experimenting with my face. I focused my gaze like a trial lawyer, poised for the kill. I raced my eyes back and forth like Hyperboy. I put on the easy smile of the Huckster. I was exposing my personas by exaggerating them. At other times, I just stared intently into my eyes. Self-discovery means that there is someone in there waiting to be discovered, right? Mostly all I saw was a nervous little boy. Was he my destiny? Or was there another self waiting at the tail end of this worry horse? Where to find my original face?

I became quite paranoid, imagining that everything was about me. When the bank teller was unfriendly, I took it personally. If my best friend didn't call me back the same day, an arrow to the heart. When my horse lost by a nose, the universe was sending me a sign. Drowning in my own shame, I began to walk on eggshells everywhere I went, *persona non grata* on Mother Earth and in my own skin. I waited to be outed for the fraud that I was.

It became difficult for me to make a living in this condition. Before, my pumped-up Huckster persona was completely undeterred by rejection, but in this highly sensitive state, I experienced sales refusals like a bite to the hand. For years I had chastised my reluctant brother because he wouldn't door-knock, and now I understood. He had actually been truer to himself—I had been a master of disguise. Yet how can one survive the battlefield without armor?

After some time, I stumbled into a still darker abyss. Here, my compass was unreadable. The identities that had been my guideposts were nowhere to be found. I had deconstructed the beliefs and structures that had given me direction, but I had yet to unfold new myths in their place. Without even a rudimentary sense of who I was, I didn't know how to interpret experience. What was my framework of interpretation? Who was the watcher, the interpreter, the interpreted? Whose eyes did I look at myself through?

Lost in uncharted territory, I began to panic. I had worked so hard to get away from a life of torment, and here I was again—only this time I was the one who opened the door and locked me in. I was relatively intact when I began. Now I was crossing the street to avoid people, and I couldn't quite remember what day it was. I wanted to trust this unfolding, but had I pushed off from myself too far?

The Warrior jumped in the ring to knock me back to my senses. He prodded me to give up on this painful adventure and get back into the courtroom. Little Missy jumped in the ring to defend my choices. They dodged and weaved for weeks:

> **Warrior:** Come on, enough is enough. So you have issues? So what? The most successful men use their pain as a motivator. Put your energy back into the courtroom. Make yourself useful.

> **Little Missy:** Don't confuse success with adaptation. Look at who succeeds. Often it is those who are running from the truth the fastest. Their fame distracts them from their shame. It is a big cover-up. You can't have outer truth without inner truth. Have the courage to stay with this unraveling. Express old anger. Cry the tears of truth. Peel the layers of pain. Go *shuck* yourself.

> **W:** Haven't you suffered enough in your lifetime? Why drown in the long ago? You're a man of action, and the courtroom is your true home. Get back now before the opportunity passes. Craft a better life for yourself.

> **LM:** *Craft a better self for your life.* Have faith in your choices. You're trying to shape a truer life. Hang in there.

Although Little Missy put up a brave front, she was on slippery ground. After months in ungrounded territory, I longed to feel solid. For better or worse, I still associated masculinity with solidity. I had grown up with my male role models staring at me from the television screen. When the Fonz struggled to admit he was wrong, I admired him. Vulnerability was the enemy. Just put on your weight belt, squat down, and move those heavy feelings off to the side. There are far more important things to be done.

I weighed their messages for weeks. I could start a practice and put all this old pain away until my career ends. By then I would be too tired to delve into it—a perfect plan! Why not? What kind of fool chooses to suffer? My peers had issues, but they were out in the world making things happen. What did they know that I didn't? Was I just more damaged? Were they just more masked? Can you live an authentic life out of touch with the trauma buried below? Can you be both successful *and* emotionally healthy?

The School of Heart Knocks

Although the body travels forward chronologically, one's emotional consciousness lingers at any point of departure. If you were one of the rare few who remained intact throughout childhood, then and now remain united. But if you are like most of us, some part of you was left behind on the journey. If all you seek is survival, then it's probably wise to leave it back there. But if you really want to live, it's imperative that you go back down the path and claim it. You've got to *be there then* before you can *be here now.* The mystery begins with our history.

My physical memories and emotions were generally segregated from each other, which meant that most of my emotional lifeline had not been integrated into consciousness. In a way, I felt like an a-historical zombie wandering through someone else's life.

I left my long-time therapist. As I attempted to become more connected to my emotional landscape, the lack of resonance between us became more evident. She represented who I had been but not who I was becoming. I needed a therapist who lived closer to the emotional bone.

I soon found Marika. A seasoned professor at *the school of heart knocks*, Marika listened with her heart first. A master of the art of presence, she modeled equanimity to me at a time when I needed it most. She was the perfect container to hold my brokenness safe.

With this relationship as launching pad, I revisited my childhood, beginning at the hospital where I was born. I visited old homes, schools, bakeries, racetracks, people I knew. I walked old neighborhoods for hours at a time. I sat on old park benches. I bought and read old comic books. I went to the university library and looked through old newspaper microfiche. I listened to old music. I stared at family pictures for hours.

Wherever I was, I went for the feeling. It wasn't enough to know that I had been somewhere, I had to feel it in my bones. When I resisted, I meditated. I closed my eyes and envisioned the person or place. I kept at it until the veil came off and the emotional memory emerged. Then I would turn the page....

I remembered many moments from childhood when my attempts to express my emotions had been halted by judgment. Those releases were a quest for liberation from the weight of other people's baggage, but no one cared. Then as now, social order took precedence over emotional harmony.

While feeling was the focus, my new process of re-integration also included a strong emphasis on the thinking self. I needed to bring my mind back into the equation, grounding my feelings in a framework of self-understanding. For this purpose I began a re-integration journal. On the left side of each page I listed experiences and relationships from early life. In the center I noted some of the feelings and memories that emanated from them. On the right side, a list of the issues and patterns they had forged.

This journal was one of the most useful tools I utilized on the healing path. It was a well-intentioned use of the mind. Instead of thinking to detach, it allowed me to form bridges between my emotional experiences and my cognitive understanding of those experiences.

Too many of us move through our lives with our true selves buried below layers of repressed emotion. With so much energy channeled toward sustaining the repression, there is little left over for the deeper questions. The consequences of our evasion are profound. Our stock-piles toxify into a cache of weapons that turn inward against the self: *quick fix, long suffering*. As Rumi said, "Most people guard against the fire, and so end up in it." This is *the power of then*. If we don't deal with our stuff, it deals with us.

Shadow Boxing

One night, I made the decision to practice. I set my alarm and drove to the Law Society early in the morning. I pulled into the underground to park and turned off the car. But my moment of certainty had passed. Frustrated, I hit the dashboard hard. What is the big deal? For God's sake, it's just a job!

I climbed the stairs up to the Law Society. I stared at the building. I stared at the door. I couldn't open it. It was as though two masses of earth were pushing up against each other inside me. Neither would give way. I lay down in a nearby park.

I was at the edge of two differing realities. The door to one was fifteen yards from the patch of grass I lay on and led straight into the heart of traditional society. The other door led to an unknown wilderness of meaning. Its nature would unfold as I walked. What was the criterion for choosing between them? I wracked my brain for an answer.

I decided to go for a walk. Lose the day but honor my soul? As I walked, I found myself glorifying the people who walked hurriedly by, like they were going somewhere important—what did they know that I didn't? I took a ferry to Toronto Island where I sat near the lake and watched the swans, pure and white. They seemed to know why they were here. I meditated on one question: What is a life fully lived? Many answers floated past me—power, freedom, achievement, security, goodness, wisdom, love. Each had its merits, but my thoughts kept coming back to the same answer: *meaning*. A life fully lived is filled with genuine meaning.

In and of itself, this did not resolve my confusion. The question transformed: What has meaning for *me*? Did law have meaning for me? It felt like an old path that I knew well, but I wasn't sure it had meaning anymore. And what of the hazy other path? Little Missy was inviting me to believe that it would become clearer after the suffering. A pot of gold at the end of the *pain-bow*? I looked at the swans and wondered—could I trust my pain to liberate me after it had imprisoned me most of my life?

That night I looked in the mirror for a long time. What do you feel? What is your intuition? An answer slowly emerged. It was just a sensation, but it had a quiet power. It invited me to wait. Just wait. I had a strange faith in it. I abandoned the idea of practicing law, yet again.

4 Refuge

In order to create a solid foundation, we have to sort out the roots of our childhood. Where the ground was inhospitable, we need to transplant our psyche to more fertile soil. This involves paying attention to the environments we live in and the ground we create around us.

— ANODEA JUDITH

Although something felt wrongheaded about it, I enrolled in a long-distance master's degree program at Saybrook Graduate School in San Francisco. Saybrook is one of the few humanistic psychology programs in the U.S. Here I could study Maslow to my soul's content.

As I began my studies I was again reminded of the relentlessness of my early issues. Whenever I sat down to write, I felt anxious and distracted. The nature of my anxiety pointed right back to my trauma history: a fear of homelessness, a state of hyper-vigilance.

I soon began to have dream after dream about the comforts of home. In one dream, I walked into a little Hansel and Gretel cottage and felt uncommonly safe and sound. I smelled bread baking, and there was a stew piping-hot on the stove-top. In another, I was in a cozy attic writing poetry with a woman peacefully asleep on the bed beside me. These were images of home that I had surely never known.

I got the hint. In Maslow's hierarchy of needs, your safety needs (security, protection, stability, and order) have to be gratified before you can move organically on to higher considerations. I had never really gratified these needs in childhood. My sense of security was undermined by evictions and by my mother's repeated assertion that I wasn't welcome in my own home (she, too, had grown up unrooted). Although I had lived away from the family for eight years, I was haunted by these memories. I still came home to my own apartment expecting an eviction notice.

I flew to San Francisco for my first Saybrook residential conference. While in the air, I realized that I might have acted too soon. As the plane hit mild turbulence over Utah, I felt disproportionately afraid. Without a solid core, flying can be a terrifying experience. I was getting a message: *Forget graduate school for now. You are trying to honor this calling too early. If you step on the right path at the wrong time, you have stepped on the wrong path. Go home.*

I resisted. Why should I have to bow to a neurotic need? Why can't I find a sense of stability in my own skin? We hit another wave of turbulence. I felt terrified. All I could think about was a house I had seen just before I left. The message was now crystal clear: *Until you feel safe in the world, you won't find your essential home. Neurotic or not, go back and buy that house!*

I landed at the airport, paid the change fee, and flew right back home on the night flight. Two days later, I bought my first house and withdrew from Saybrook. Later that week, I bought a puppy and named him Maslow, a noisy reminder of a calling that was waiting somewhere ahead.

The Spiritual Bypass

Signing up for Saybrook was my first experience with what is often called the spiritual bypass. The bypass is the tendency to jump to spirit prematurely, usually in an effort to avoid various aspects of earthly reality. Those realities can include any form of discomfort, economic pressure, or emotional distress. Anything we want to trip out of.

In a world of pain, the spiritual bypass is an ongoing temptation. It gives us something to believe in and a vision of what we are missing in our localized reality. Without it, many of us would have to suffer unbearable situations. At the same time, it can be a detour on the path to genuine spirituality. In our efforts to leapfrog to something better, we often avoid something crucial. Spirit becomes the crutch rather than an expression of a natural unfolding.

"Spirituality" is just another word for reality. The most spiritual person lives in *all* aspects of reality simultaneously — the emotional, the material, and the subtle realms.

Although appearing spiritual, bypassers are actually cut off from various aspects of reality. By turning away from old pain, they shackle themselves with their unresolveds. With their head in the clouds, they cannot see where they are walking. This may be a temporary tool for survival, but real growth demands that we come back down to earth and face our demons. We have to grow down to grow up.

I had one friend who bypassed by studying heady spiritual texts. He talked a good spirit game, but when you looked into his eyes there was no one home.

I dated a woman who wore high heels at all times. I asked why and she replied, "When I get close to the ground, I feel all my suffering. This way I am a little bit closer to God and free of pain." Whenever she said, "It's all good," I could see in her eyes that it was actually all *bad*.

Of course, it is not easy to identify a bypass from the act itself. What you do to bypass reality, someone else will do to confront it. It's all a matter of intention, and only you can know your intention. In this case, I was bypassing in an effort to avoid doing more painstaking work around my basic needs. I wanted the relief of my highest callings before I had built the foundation to support them.

Feathering My Nest

When I walked into my new house, I had my first taste of rootedness. My shoulders dropped. My root chakra relaxed. It was a lovely and peaceful feeling. The feeling only deepened when I installed a house alarm and arranged disability insurance. I felt safe for the first time in my life.

My dear grandfather visited me and sat in my dining room crying. He too had lost a house. Sitting quietly beside him, I felt tremendous relief. I had carried the weight of his failures on my shoulders as well.

After a few days in the house, I began to settle into profound exhaustion. Like a soldier returning from years on a foreign battlefield, all I wanted to do was sleep. How had I lived in such an exhausted state? What had carried me along? Who held me safe?

Soon a new calmness descended upon me and settled into my bones. Along with it came a more stable framework of perception. The world around me looked less cold. I felt like someone who had a right to be here.

I gained insight into my security issues, beginning with my relationship history. I recognized why I had almost always had a girlfriend. They were the only refuge I had ever known. They rooted me to Mother Earth.

I also recognized what was missing in my recent efforts to clear my debris. Although I had begun to surrender to my feelings, I often did so like the Warrior—refusing comforts, shelter, and a good night's sleep. In just a few weeks in my own home, it was evident that a place of refuge allowed my processes of emotional clearing to happen with more fluidity and grace. Issues emerged, but there was something to ground them.

After only a few weeks in my little refuge, I began to grumble for more. In Maslow's theory of human motivation, development is governed by a hierarchy of needs. Our most basic needs are physiological, such as hunger and sleep. These are followed by the needs for safety, belongingness, and love. Then comes the need to be esteemed and, finally, self-actualization. Once we have gratified a need, our actualizing tendency motivates us to satisfy the next stage in the hierarchy.

One of the indicators of a readiness to move higher is a certain restlessness. Maslow named this "grumble theory." He encouraged us to understand our frustration not as a negative thing but as a harbinger of change. It may be a sign that our current consciousness is struggling to break through to the next stage of growth.

This way of thinking is in many ways inimical to the feel-good teachings of Western culture. When we struggle, we are often encouraged to put on a happy face and get back in the game. Maslow invites us to delve deeper and consider the possibility that our frustration has something valuable to teach us.

Although I had managed to survive economically for years, I had done so as an edgy door-knocker. This served its purpose, but the desperate and artificial energy of the door-knock held me in a kind of peripheral, uncivilized way of being. After a selling phase, it might take weeks to calm down and find center—the Huckster's mask stuck like crazy glue. When you're singing for your supper, you don't care about much else. But when you feel more secure, you begin to notice that something is missing. I began to grumble for a more civilized way to secure a living.

I stayed up late one night wondering what to do: How can I convert this part-time hustle into a real business?

Early in the morning I fell asleep, only to be awakened by a dream. In it, a small woman was walking down a subdivision street putting green fliers in the doors. I had the oddest feeling that she was Little Missy. The flier had pictures of my window products set out in orderly fashion. It was packed with details and prices in all the ways that marketers warn against. I spent the better part of the morning constructing the flier, then spent the rest of the week constructing a subdivision mapping system and hiring a crew of flier deliverers. Within two weeks, I was swamped with callers. I hired my brother to install and a friend to sell for me. As quick as that, I did not have to hustle to earn a living.

I began to rely more on my dreams as directors and harbingers of change. I couldn't rely on them as a child because they were too muddled to interpret. There were still too many things I didn't want to know. Yet now that I was calming and clarifying my inner world, my dreams were becoming more transparent. The messages still dared not emerge during the day but waited until my defenses were asleep. Soul-speak.

Although they were still hazy, I was forming stronger images of my dream weaver, Little Missy. I saw her dropping essential hints into the river wild while my defenses slept. She strode ahead, she sat on my shoulder, she lingered within at the fork in the river of (un)consciousness. Perhaps I was not as alone as I thought.

Next Stop, Buddhaland

Just as I was beginning to recognize the presence of one guardian angel, I lost the most precious one I had ever known.

It was a winter's day and I felt a pull toward my grandfather. I left my chores and drove to his apartment. I found him sitting in his favorite chair, apparently talking to someone off to the side, though there was no one there. I had the sense that my Beela was readying to leave us. We had a gentle conversation about his concern for the well-being of everyone in the family. The next morning, I woke to the call that he had passed.

After learning of his death, I went to see him. He had not been taken by the funeral home yet, so we had some time together. As I sat beside him, my connection to Essence unexpectedly deepened. Cut to the core by his passing, I felt my layers of artifice and conditioning fall momentarily away as a broader universe of perception revealed itself to me, enveloped me, soothed me. Suddenly I knew no distinction between him, me, the sunlight that flooded the room. It was all the same. In the words of *Hakomi* pioneer Ron Kurtz, I had entered a place we might call *Buddhaland*. The frivolousness of my waking concerns and those of the culture around me was instantly revealed.

I drove slowly home and felt saddened at what I saw around me—newspapers that commodified fear, people racing about in search of something they already had.

When I got back to the house, I put on a disc that I had once judged as too New Age flaky for my liking: Aeoliah's *Angel Love*. What I experienced as ungrounded when I was in a pragmatic state of mind sounded like God's work in this more timeless space. I lay on my bedroom floor and listened to it on repeat. With rare openness, I deepened into the sounds of angels lovingly floating my Beela up to heaven. I felt his presence in the music. I felt him within me and I felt him around me, and in that moment I didn't know the difference. Is there a difference? How to separate the alive and the dead from the perspective of Essence?

My grandmother called and asked me to write his eulogy for the morning funeral. But how, Bubbi? He is still so alive to me. I lay on the floor for hours, wondering how to eulogize the spirit that lives on.

A practical voice shouted: "Get to it! Will your Beela be buried without a eulogy?" (Jewish guilt.) I opened the computer, and slowly words found their way onto the page. About halfway through I nodded off. Before a moment could pass, the rear door motion light came on and woke me. I looked out. Nothing there. I went back to work and soon fell asleep. Again, the motion light woke me. I had been at this desk for hours, and the light only came on in the moments after I drifted off. I finished page three and my eyes were closing fast. Yet again the light came on. Again I looked outside. There was nothing there to trigger it. I had the distinct sense that I was being awakened for a reason. Toward the end, I wrote the following words of gratitude:

> "There was a quote that guided me over so many hurdles during the last fifteen years. It was in a book I was reading as an undergraduate. The quote was 'The light shines in the darkness and the darkness cannot overcome it.' Until now, the author was anonymous. But not anymore. I know who wrote it, and more importantly, I know who showed me the truth of it—Beela."

Not a moment later, the motion light came back on.

I read the eulogy the next morning. I had often been very anxious speaking before groups, but I had no such anxiety that day. The illusion of separateness that fueled my anxiety had fallen away. I was floating in golden light, cracked open to a seamless and peaceful universe of meaning. As I spoke, I imagined a bridge from Beela's spirit to mine, and I saw gifts floating across it in my direction. He had continued to fill me up with his loving kindness for thirty-three years, and now that my tanks were filled, he went on his way.

In the following few weeks, I continued to float through this Buddhaland of strangely radiant perception. I felt like an enhanced version of myself, tapped into a magical realm that both transcended and sourced my usual awareness. The most mundane moments seemed somehow perfect. There were still the chores and unpaid bills, but they were lost in something bigger, more meaningful. People who had seemed negative before looked beautiful to me and intrinsic to my being. Even walking to the corner store became a fascinating experience, one eye on the road ahead and another on the heavens above. No difference. It was all part of the same giant swirl of light.

My Beela's death had given me a glimpse of life as it ought to be— clear, unified, radiant, essential. Each time that motion light came on and startled me back to work, it shed light on the dynamic nature of universal connectivity. In that moment, I knew that I did not swim alone. Some force swam beside me, above me, and within me, insisting that I complete my task. I summoned it, it summoned me, separate voices inextricably woven through a choir of unified light, each looking out for the other. We were in this together. We were *this* together.

I knew that this Buddhaland was the way home. I couldn't quite reconcile its unified nature with the idea of individual path, but I sensed that somewhere at its heart were messages about my own unfolding—where to walk, what to do, who to love.

The challenge was staying here. Peak experiences crack us open and give us a glimpse of the possible, but the trick is to master those issues and challenges that keep us from living there full-time. In my usual frame of mind, I would have attributed the motion light to meaningless coincidence, as I always did when I bumped into someone I had thought of just a moment earlier. Struggling to meet basic needs and challenges, my canvas could not accommodate the bigger picture.

Although I hungered to swim here forever, I knew that I wasn't ready. I had been transformed and I would keep this learning close to my heart, but there was much work to be done first. Miles to go before I could sleep. Miles to go before I could really swim with God.

The Universal Broadcasting System

Whether we consciously know it or not, we are all subscribers to the Universal Broadcasting System. The UBS is the dynamic and benevolent network of relatedness that brings lessons and messengers onto our path in an eternal effort to grow our soul to the next stage of consciousness. The universe presents us with endless opportunities to synchronize our path with our truth.

At its helm is the divine Mother herself, busily orchestrating the symphony of our lives. In her dynamic universe, there is always work to be done. We are brought down this road or that, tripped up by an unexpected illness, bumped into someone who has something to teach us, walked into a soul-mate just before we marry someone else, all by a Mother with a benevolent intention: the growth of the individual and collective soul.

Supporting her efforts is our own personal dream team—our inner voice, our guiding angels, our silent friends. Masters of the wake-down call, they refuse to turn the alarm off until we have opened our eyes.

If we choose to participate in our unfolding, we slowly become our own beacon of light. Where most of us only summon a few localized "coincidences" now and then, our powerful lighthouse begins to emit an entirely different signal. The whole system gets busy with us. We summon the lessons, the lessons summon us. Pretty soon, we cannot distinguish ourselves from what we have summoned. We see a web of benevolent intentionality everywhere we look, serendipity galore.

The UBS goes underground unless we do the work to keep it airborne. If we choose to resist our opportunities, its protection will fade, and the lessons may get more and more insidious. Although the system is benevolently intended, it is hardly painless. Suffering is one of its primary tools of expansion.

Punch Drunk (*Candida Albicans* and Food Sensitivities)

Was it doubted that those who corrupt
their own bodies conceal themselves?

—WALT WHITMAN

While floating to the corner store one afternoon, I began to feel un-comfortable. I had visited Buddhaland for as long as I could manage at this stage of my awakening. I reached the corner store and headed straight for the ice cream. A man on a mission, I bought a tub of but-terscotch and a big bag of cookies.

I walked home and ate my treats with determination. Sweet wheat, bring me back to the world I know! Shut me down! Fill me up! Turn off the tap of Essence!

After a few days watching numbing videos and eating sugary treats, I lost my connection to Buddhaland. Everything became sepa-rate again. I had returned to the Earth I knew best.

My new girlfriend encouraged me to make an appointment to have my food sensitivities tested. She thought that my tendency to shut myself down with certain foods was linked to a sensitivity to those foods. I was skeptical. Maybe life circumstances and emotional debris could block the path, but food?

The results seemed to support her view. I registered sixty-three severe food allergies. They included wheat, dairy, sugar, and caffeine. Of particular importance, my *Candida albicans* score was very high. A fungus, *Candida albicans* is naturally present in the body. If it grows out of control, it can inhibit enzyme production and cause yeast infec-tions, bloatedness, confusion, exhaustion, low libido, loss of memory, and a feeling of drunkenness. It can basically take over your life.

Everything I read resonated with my history. I had felt listless for nearly five years. I woke up feeling lethargic and felt tired throughout the day. My face and body were bloated, my eyes yellow and blurry, and my libido was diminished. I often had brain fog. Sometimes I walked to the corner store and forgot what I was supposed to buy.

I embarked on a healing journey. I began taking digestive enzymes and doing parasite cleanses. I took acidophilus to improve the ratio of good to bad bacteria in my body. I went for regular colonics to clear excessive yeast from my digestive system. I tried to avoid my allergens.

At first it was impossible. I couldn't stop eating the foods that were worst for me. The body craves what it's used to. If healthy, it craves healthy. If unhealthy, it craves unhealthy. I was clearly unhealthy.

The cycle was a vicious one. For instance, I would eat pasta and become sluggish. Then I would have a coffee to wake me up. My adrenals would crash and then I would crave another coffee to help me recover from the effects of the last one. When that didn't work, I ate candy. Then I would crash again, and crave comfort food. One allergen led to another led to another....

The most startling observation was the relationship between candida and my emotional state. When the candida got really high, I became emotionally unpredictable and easily triggered. Old memories and feelings rose to the surface, and it became difficult to distinguish the past from the present.

Accepting my condition, I went back to the cleanse with a vengeance. I began to fast twice a week. On fasting days I drank only water and fresh vegetable juices. On the other days, I ate a light *vegaquarian* diet: vegetables and fish only. I starved the candida, which feed on sugars and starches.

After a few months on this more extreme diet, I stopped laboring through my days. With a bounce in my step, I began to feel curious about life again. I looked out at trees and really *saw* them. My feelings were connected to the moment itself, rather than the befuddled remnants of past events. Purifying my body had purified my outlook.

Seeking a Little Soulitude

Once again, this degree of openness became unbearable. As I ventured out to do my chores, I felt overwhelmed by the city. It was not unlike the way one feels after receiving a massage and then walking onto a busy city street. I felt too vulnerable for the world.

I began to crave the yeast-friendly foods I had been addicted to. I needed to turn myself off, again, and my body knew exactly where to look. These cravings illustrated the complex nature of my relationship with food. At very high levels, candida and food sensitivities surely had a life of their own, but this wasn't the whole story.

Like all of us, I lived in a *habitual range of e-motion,* the particular degree of aliveness that I was comfortable with. In this instance, I turned to food to armor myself against feeling and to alter my consciousness. It wasn't a physiological addiction. It was an addiction to self-distraction. I gravitated toward agitating foods to bring me back into range.

Our habitual range of e-motion can be defined as our emotional comfort zone. It is that place between vulnerability and armor that we return to time and again. For some of us it is an open and vital range. For others, it is narrow and tight. Most of us go back to the range that kept us safe during inclement weather, often without recognizing that it has outlived its usefulness. Home, home on the range.

To move forward, we must identify our habitual range and the ways that we bring ourselves back in range. Examples of the latter can include betraying a love relationship before we get too close, or sabotaging a great achievement just before it is done. When we remove one habit, we often replace it with another so that we can stay in range.

At the core of my limited range were fears around vulnerability. I was pushing the range by creating the conditions for a more vulnerable reality but sabotaging it at the same time. This was yet another reminder that if I wanted to live a soulful life, I needed to do more healing and build a stronger inner foundation.

As I closed down, I felt very sad. I decided to go to the country for some time alone in nature. Perhaps a more spacious landscape would be more inviting?

In the city, just a few minutes of driving made my breath shallow and closed my heart. I put on New Age music to keep me open, but it felt laughably incongruent with the harshness of city life. I switched to Top 40. How to float in golden light when startled by car horns?

Yet on a country highway miles from the city, that donut craving that nagged at me on the drive through the city lost its voice. I began to wonder if my habitual range of e-motion was the only obstacle to openness back home. What about urban life itself?

The moment I walked through the cottage door, the scent of pine wood dropped me deeper into my body. The first thing I noticed was the exhaustion that I hadn't noticed back in the city. I lay down on the wood floor and fell fast asleep.

After waking, I stayed on the floor and felt into myself. There were many tight places. I began to breathe consciously, deeply, into my center. I wanted more space inside. I stayed inside the cottage for a full day, alternating sleeps with purifying breath and movement. Expelling the bad breath, breathing anew. Natural medicine. By the time I left the cottage, I was ready to open.

As I walked alone in the spacious forest, I was reminded of how easy it can be to stay open. Here my senses sprang to life. A cacophony of bird calls invited me to listen and reminded me that I was not alone. In the city, I often felt alone. My spirit couldn't merge with fast-moving cars and neon lights. A master of unity *un*consciousness, I separated to preserve myself. But there was no reason to separate from a forest that welcomed me like an old friend.

As I wandered aimlessly, I felt the presence of the Buddhaland that I had fled not so long ago. I felt it come closer now and then, like a butterfly that comes in and out of our field of vision, reminding us that a more vibrant universe of perception is waiting in the wings. We may not see it, but it always has us in its sights.

After a few days, I entered Buddhaland. Here was only open and more open, and I walked heart-long down deeper pathways of perception. I saw all things within me, and myself in all things, and marveled at the seamlessness of this unified world. How perfect it all is!

Although I had gone through many changes over these last months, Buddhaland felt unchanged, permanent, timeless. It was as if I had never left this place and it had never left me, despite my immersion in more mundane concerns. If I wanted to touch it, I just had to get out from under the obstructions that blinded me to what was always before me.

Soulitude, undistracted time alone with my soul-self, was clearly essential to my journey. No amount of massage, yoga classes, or lazy beach days could compare to its regenerative qualities.

Where Wired Is Required

I drove back to the city curious as to how I could stay open. If I couldn't stay open where I lived, how could I possibly find true-path?

The temptation to close began even before I got home. I managed to stay within myself for most of the drive, but when I turned onto a highway about thirty miles from downtown Toronto, I felt myself pick up the pace. The speed limit was the same, but the energy was more intense. I began to think about coffee. Should I pull over and get one? I contained the impulse, but within moments I was driving even faster as my breathing began to get shallow and my body tightened.

The traffic slowed down due to an accident on the side of the road. We all just had to look. I wondered why—because we are voyeurs, or because we crave something real to bring us back to center?

When I entered the city I felt afraid. Re-entry trauma? I pulled onto a side street to center myself before driving downtown, but there was a ticket cop walking in my direction. I looked up and realized that I was stopped in a no-standing zone: "It's not like the woods, Jeffrey. You can't just pull over and contemplate your navel."

I pulled back onto the roadway without noticing the school bus that was chugging along beside me. The message was communicated loud and clear by the angry driver: "There are children on this bus, you selfish ass!" Message received. What is healthy self-awareness on a walk in the country is dangerous self-absorption in the city. Forget the Bambi routine—armor up, or else.

Inside my house, I settled back into myself. But I couldn't hide in my house forever. I lived in this urban culture, and I needed to know if I could live a growth-full life here: What turns off the tap of Essence? What keeps it open? Do I close because I have issues with my own boundaries, or does the culture itself necessitate it? How to deal with over-stimulation if you are not emotionally numb?

Out in the city, everything seemed to conspire to close me down. When I turned onto a main street, I was bombarded by cars, faces, white noise, the inhumane pace of modern life. Again, my breath went shallow. It hurt to breathe all this in. I soon craved starchy foods and caffeinated drinks, walking that strange line between numbing the over-stimulation and increasing my pace to meet it. Often I would find myself buying things that could bring me no real pleasure. When small things lost their novelty, I longed for bigger ones. *Unconscious consumerism preys on the uncentered.* Once we lose touch with our center, we don't know who we are anymore, and marketers fill the void by telling us who we ought to be. The quick fix is big business. But substitute gratifications don't satisfy us. If they did, we wouldn't keep craving more of them.

After a few weeks of cultural overload, I lost all connection to the person who had come into his own in the spacious countryside. Hemmed in and hyped up, my imagination stagnated. My body slouched. My eyes stopped looking up when I walked.

I went right back to the country to find my way back to center. At this immature stage of expansion, escape still seemed like my best hope. As I sat before landscapes that were spacious and inviting, I was able to meet myself again.

In my reflections, I wondered how to bridge these seemingly incongruent worlds. When I wanted an externalized life, Western culture was the perfect place to be. Yet as I began to orient toward the inner temple, the limitations of mainstream culture became painfully obvious. How to stay tenderly soulful in the heart of an overwhelming culture?

Journeys to Spacious Landscapes

For me, frequent trips to spacious landscapes became the beacon of light to which I compared my urban experience. Souljourns. In the city many of us lose contact with the bigger picture quite easily. The concreteness of the outer world concretizes our inner world. Soon there is no space to meet ourselves: narrow streets, narrow imaginings.

In the country, we can open to a more spacious reality: broad vistas, broad imaginings. The space outside invites us to open inside, until there is no distinction between inner and outer.

In the city, I developed a keen eye for the signs that I was losing sight of the light: constant agitation, cynicism, worried thinking. I would find my way to the countryside whenever the signs reappeared. Back in nature I would clear the emotional and cultural debris that I had accumulated, finding my way back to a spacious inner narrative. These journeys became even more essential as I began to put more energy into excavating my callings.

I encourage you to find those landscapes that coax your soul out of hiding and invite you into your fullness. Find ways to visit them as often as possible. It is nice to strive for a spacious reality right where you live, but in the meantime....

Over the next months, I went back and forth between city and country in an effort to clarify my lessons. Must I do like Thoreau and live simply in a distant wood, or could I stay open in the city with a little practice? Parts of me still wanted to believe that where one lived wasn't essential. It was all about how you lived, finding refuge within, that sort of thing. Surely there are people who live deeply soulful lives in the heart of the city?

Or maybe certain landscapes are more appropriate for certain individuals? Does the soul not have a preference? And what of past lives? Does our soul not demand a return to old stomping grounds?

Although I was beginning to make inroads into the next stage of my soul's journey, my attachment to the familiar—the gritty urban marketplace, the ways of the city lawyer, an armored way of being— was still very powerful. Moving to the spacious countryside was not yet a real possibility. I still had essential lessons to learn right here, and I knew it.

Boundary-Making

As I sought to stay soulful in the city, establishing healthy boundaries became my primary focus.

The first stage of boundary-making was awareness. I began by paying close attention to my moment-by-moment interface with everything around me: Where did I begin and the other end? What environments and circumstances shifted the boundary? In what situations did I lose my sense of self?

Everywhere, I watched. At the racetrack, I watched to see how my betting choices were influenced by the changing tides of the odds. Could I stand my ground and bet my instinctive choice, or was I influenced by the perceptions of the crowd? If in a mall at Christmas, did I get sucked in and buy needlessly? If friends wanted to spend time with me one evening, did I let their desires negate my own plans? At what point did I get lost in the herd?

I noticed an inextricable connection between breath and boundaries. When I breathed strongly and evenly, I experienced a sense of my individuality. When my breath became shallow, my awareness of myself became tenuous.

With my breath in my holster, I deliberately ventured into overwhelming environments such as edgy bars and busy buses. I watched for signs that I was losing contact with my boundaried self and invited myself to breathe through the overwhelm.

This practice made me stronger at the edges. It also validated my existence. By breathing through my discomfort, I was implicitly saying, "I matter," until I began to actually believe it.

To let go of duality, we must first establish our separateness. To find out who we are, we must learn where we end and the other begins. As a general rule, if we are too rigid, we are over-boundaried. Imprisoned behind a wall of armor, there is no way for anything to touch us. But if we are too malleable, we are boundary-less. We are just a vessel for the world to fill. People with healthy boundaries tend to live somewhere in between. They have the capacity for both assertiveness and surrender at all times. When they do move toward one polarity, they do so with intentionality. They *choose* to surrender, *choose* to assert. In all cases, their sense of self remains intact.

After two years, this refuge phase of my journey ended. With a sense of physical home under my belt, my orientation now shifted toward the more challenging matter of my spiritual home—the quest for true-path. In a survivalist culture, you are only homeless if you have no shelter. Through the eyes of Essence, you are only homeless if you are not honoring your karmic code for this lifetime.

5 Befriending Confusion

You must have chaos within to
give birth to a dancing star.

—Friedrich Nietzsche

The shift began while I slept. I dreamt that I was a trial lawyer on the verge of victory in a murder trial. As I sat in my office at night writing the jury address, I heard a knock at the door. In came an angelic young girl who sat down at the desk and just stared at me and smiled. I went back to the jury address. When I began reading it to the jury the next morning, I found myself reading a short story that I had actually written in high school. The story was about a peaceful boy who loved to write. I had always loved this story.

This singular dream opened the floodgates of confusion. Every night was riddled with nightmares about my path. I was the lawyer, writer, psychologist, the homeless man in a bus shelter. The confusion spread to the daylight hours. Conflicting images were strewn all across my inner landscape. The spiritual *emergingcy* that had briefly overwhelmed me years before had returned with a vengeance.

The Place of Not Knowing

I sensed that Little Missy was in the heart of it. Who else could have taken the wrapping off all this confusion? The projectionist in my theatre of uncertainty, she floated possibilities on the screen before me.

I spent the next few months grasping for any path that offered relief. My monkey mind converted the question of identity into a detached exercise, actively weighing the pros and cons of every possibility: Which path has more advantages? Fewer risks? Total them all up and there you go.

Of course, this got me nowhere. The questions of spiritual identity are not math problems. They are existential inquiries of a heartfelt nature.

One particular dream hit me deep. In it I was sitting peacefully at the back of a coffee shop, avidly writing in a notepad. I woke in the morning with the compulsion to write a short story. The text moved out of me as if pre-written, as though that writer who lived restlessly inside me wrote it as I slept.

But after a few days of pen to paper, I lost contact with the writer within. I could sense him there, on the other side of the proverbial glass, but I couldn't quite touch him. I recognized that this was no writer's block. It was actually the resistance that emerges when you step on the right path at the wrong time. Your feet stop moving until you turn back to the paths that need to be walked first. How many times would I have to learn this lesson? (Many.)

The emergingcy intensified. Sleepless nights, teeth grinding, inexplicable anger. New pathways were screaming for space, old pathways were digging in their heels. The peanut gallery was truly nuts. Pitter pattern, pitter pattern....

I soon longed for the path I knew best—trial law. The Warrior still had a superhero's grip on my psyche, and he kept calling out to me. Around this time, Eddie Greenspan left me a telephone message. He wanted to have lunch. A sign?

Before meeting him, I went to a downtown courthouse and watched a criminal lawyer cross-examine a witness. The lawyer danced with the witness for hours, and I was right there with him, magnetically drawn to every nuance. I left the court with the certainty that I would practice law.

I brought lunch to Eddie's office. He talked about the trials he was working on, the challenges of his day. As he answered one phone call after another, I felt into the sense of urgency, the intensity, the excitement. I imagined the prizes that came with the game: money, security, the satisfaction of doing valuable work, all the spoils of war.

After lunch, I lay down on a grassy knoll. It felt so good to have an answer. No more confusion. No more aimlessness. Who are you, really? I am a trial lawyer, a modern-day litigation warrior.

I was soon interrupted by a little voice: "Do you really want this? Is this meaningful for you? Do you really covet these prizes anymore?" I ignored the voice and walked determinedly to the Law Society, where I gathered the forms to open a practice.

Before I got home, the little voice was back: "If you do this now, you will never know who you really are."

Damn the little voice that was my own.

Baring Witness

When I got home, I raged at Little Missy. She tempted me off the marked trail with hints of something truer, and then drowned me in the quicksand of uncertainty.

I threw my hands up to the sky and asked for guidance. The little voice that was my own told me to get out of town for the weekend. Something was wanting to be unearthed. The next morning I drove to the woods and hiked away from civilization. As I walked I heard from Little Missy, knocking again at my door with those damn soul-guide cookies:

> Growing is all about leaps into the seeming unknown. Before you can find your way home, you must linger in the place of not knowing. Stay here until the next step organically arises. Sit until the questions that need to be lived show themselves. By surrendering to the unknown, you create the space for a deeper knowing to emerge.

> Befriend your confusion. Don't be fooled by its chaotic appearance—this is good confusion. It's a sign that your soul is in transition. Welcome it as a friend that has come from far away to bring you home. Be open to it. Keep it close.

My guiding angel often presented ideas ahead of my waking consciousness. I went back home and resisted her ideas. Perhaps more than anything, it was difficult to trust an entity that carried a blueprint for my life that existed entirely independent of my waking consciousness. Sometimes I liked it, but often it felt indescribably eerie. How to trust a blueprint written in a foreign tongue?

After some integration time, I tried to befriend my confusion but it was intensely uncomfortable. There was something meaningfully different about this particular form of confusion. Where emotional confusion had built-in release valves such as crying or raging, my existential confusion didn't seem to resolve itself through expressive means. To get to the other side, I had to hold to the misery without release. Yuck.

My *Inner Witness* rose to the fore. The Inner Witness is the detached observer that watches our experience without judgment. In moments of real stuckness, I turned to the Witness to help me see my patterns from a distance. Although I would later recognize the perils of too much Witness—we can get too removed from our experience—he was a path-saver at this confused stage of my process. It felt safer to look before I leaped.

As I watched, I saw how many issues I had with confusion itself. It seemed to be a gathering point for many of my emotional patterns.

A childhood memory kept rising into consciousness. I had gone to a friend's house for a sleepover just before I turned thirteen. Late that night my father called to say that I had to come home. I knew he was going to beat me. Once inside the house, I made the mistake of sitting on the couch close to him. He kicked me in the head so hard that I think I almost died. Ever since, I have deeply associated confusion with death. The wild frontier always comes with a hangman.

I had similarly bad associations with the unknown. When we attempt to sit in the not knowing, we often come face to face with our own history. If our sojourns into the unknown were encouraging, we may be able to stay present until the next step in the journey reveals itself. If we have had experiences that associate the unknown with pain, we may jump ship long before.

As a child, there was always a foreboding sense around the unknown. I could trust the mystery no more than I could trust confusion. Both led to unhappy endings.

As I attempted to sit within myself, my defenses kept swimming me toward familiar ground. Often my Warrior would jump to the fore and focus my energies—don't just sit there, *do* something. Through his lens, Mystery River was luxurious and foolhardy, best reserved for children's fables. There were *real* things to be accomplished.

Sometimes I would be overcome by guilt. My mother lived from paycheck to paycheck. My father was on government disability, suffering from manic depression. My grandmother had barely enough money to get by. It seemed self-indulgent, even mean-spirited, to put my esoteric inquiries ahead of their basic needs. What kind of Jew turns his back on his family? A badboy indeed.

My mind often wandered to the critical comments made by others about my decision to postpone law: "Get it together!" "Why go to school for all those years?" "You're a flake." They touched my own self-doubt, a field filled with painful memories of my father's confusion and unactualized potential. As I circled closer to my own confusion, these comments stoked my fear that I would end up exactly like him.

Vote for Flake!

Moving forward sometimes demands that we live lost, knowingly surrendering our attachment to who we think we are, voluntarily stumbling around in the dark with little to guide us.

Unfortunately, this shapeless form is difficult to sustain in a world that pressures us into premature self-definition. We are encouraged to assume a religious and political identity before we reach an age of genuine maturity. We are pressured into choosing a career and life partner before we have explored the boundless possibilities for our lives. Our ideas of self are fed to us by corporate game artists who wear us down with their generic mantras of compliance until we identify with a socially acceptable idea of self.

How many parents worked like dogs to give their children a better life and then, when their children were pressed to choose a career path, pressured them to take the most practical route? Despite the fact that they had built the girders necessary for their children to make the heartfelt choices that they couldn't, they fell right back to fear-based thinking.

Reinforcing this attitude is negative messaging about confusion itself. Vibrant and inquisitive children are often labeled hyperactive and medicated before their hunger for adventure "gets them into trouble." Saying "I don't know" in the classroom is a mark against you. Those who walk the path of uncertainty are frequently characterized as flakes, drifters, and ironically, lost souls. Nowhere in society are we taught to distinguish growth-full from aimless confusion, nervous breakdowns from breakthroughs, habitual crisis from spiritual emergingcies. Confusion is sadly stigmatized as the mark of the "loser" without regard for the fact that one cannot come to know anything without first surrendering to the not knowing.

How many of those who had a "mid-life crisis" were reluctant to experience their confusion earlier in life? What percentage of those who partnered at twenty-one are still happily together fifteen years later? How many who committed to a career path at eighteen are hungering to explore other possibilities now?

Perhaps the seemingly "together" man next door is actually less honest and courageous—a more effective master of disguise. Perhaps the "loser" has the good sense to turn away from the falsity of a disguised life and just doesn't know where to turn in a culture that does not encourage inquiry. Perhaps the "flake" is just exploring a more challenging question that takes far longer to understand.

Imagine a travel section in the local newspaper that invites you to vacate your familiar ways of being and explore other possibilities for who you are: "San Bernardino Identity Swap: Live in someone else's shoes for a week. See if they resonate more deeply with who you really are" or "Excavate Your Callings Festival: A cornucopia of depth charges, triggers, clearings, and breakthroughs in the spacious countryside. Step out of your adapted world and explore the pathways that live below the surface of your daily life. Befriend your confusion! Come one, come all!"

In this more exploratory world, the "flake" might become the philosopher-king that every country so desperately needs, guided by the deeper knowledge that comes from years spent in the not knowing.

Out Off a Limb

After months of witnessing my retreats, I began to grumble. Looking at the map of my inner terrain was good preparation but no substitute for the hike itself. I felt ready for a more embodied experience of my confusion.

I attended a workshop at the Omega Institute in Rhinebeck, New York. Led by Omega's heartfelt corporate counsel, George Kaufman, the workshop was for lawyers looking for more meaning in their daily work. I imagined that my confusion would be resolved and I would return to law with clarity.

In between the workshop exercises, George read us poetry by Rumi. I was blown away. Rumi got it: *Confusion is a mitzvah. Resisting it is pointless. Excavate and honor your deepest truths. You have nothing to lose — everything (and nothing) to gain!*

Wrote Rumi:

> Soul serves as a cup for the juice
> > That leaves the intellect in ruins.
> That candle came and consumed me,
> > about whose flame the universe
> > flutters in total confusion.

By the end of the workshop, my call to law felt hollow and unreal. It wasn't the profession itself. It was my particular relationship to it. There was something else out there for me — something else *in* there.

On the way home, I met my girlfriend to hike in the Adirondacks. At the top of Hurricane Mountain, the gate to new insights creaked open. Little Missy was becoming bolder in her efforts to coax my entelechy into consciousness:

> You've yet to befriend your confusion. You attach to one voice at the expense of the others. If you don't befriend your confusion, you'll remain trapped between worlds — on the one hand, old ways of being ready to die; on the other, new ways of being eager to be born. The bridge is confusion. You must learn how to cross it on the way home.

Coax the voices that confuse you to the surface. Hold the space for all of them at once. Remain confused until clarity emerges on its own terms. Everything in its own time.

To help me, I worked with an image of a monkey on the move. In order to move forward, he has to let go of the vine in his hand and grab onto the next one. Because of the gap between vines, there is a moment—an abyss moment—when he is not holding onto anything. His moving forward in life depends on his capacity to linger here, to trust that he will not fall to his death while he negotiates the abyss.

Over the next weeks, I felt deeply into my hunger for trial law, my love for the psychologies, the quiet sense that one day I would write. Different feelings came up with each possibility—different satisfactions and regrets, sliding doors. Who would I become if I walked this path or that? Who would I not become? What is the criterion for choosing?

One night I dreamt that I was driving to a courthouse to do a trial. My car suddenly rose up from the highway, higher and higher, far away from the world I knew. As it climbed, I felt excited and curious, but then I panicked and jumped out of the car. I fell toward Earth. My dreamscape immediately shifted to a courtroom, and I walked through the doors to begin my trial.

Although there were many possible interpretations, I knew that my soul was revealing its comfort zone through this dream. It was comfortable with what it knew best—the ways of the Warrior advocate—and resisted other ways of being. Clearly it was not only the emotional body that had a habitual range of motion. The soul had its groove, too.

As the nature of the battle revealed itself more fully, I felt afraid of the journey ahead. My conscious mind was barely adept at interpreting psychological terrain. How could I possibly interpret the language of the soul? If we accept that the soul carries the memory of past lives, how do we know when these memories are interfacing with current experience? How can we know why we retreat from certain ways of being? Can we ever really know when parts are ready to die and others to be born?

Confusion Says ...

Suddenly law was all I could think about, dream about, imagine. I
gave in and phoned an old friend who practiced defense law in a busy
firm. He had an office I could rent and assured me that he could send
me work in the early stages. He asked me to commit that minute. I told
him I would call him back later in the day. I went upstairs and took a
nap with a smile on my face. I felt relieved to have a place somewhere.
A man on a mission again. Clarity, direction—finally.

I woke up startled, covered in sweat. I needed to write something
down: "I am lost in the wilderness because I resist being lost in the
wilderness. I stay lost because I am obsessed with being found." Blah,
blah, blah. I went for a walk in a nearby park and tried to relax. A bird
shat on my shoe. Something was afoot.

The next day, I went for long pensive walks. I tried to imagine all
my different parts sitting around the hearth, taking turns with the
talking stick. Yet only one held the stick: the Warrior. He overshad-
owed everything. As I listened to him, I envisioned a soldier lost in
the bush for many years. One day, he stumbles upon a small group of
Tibetan monks. The monks feed him and give him refuge. While they
sleep, he kills them. He doesn't kill them because they are his enemy,
but because they threaten to soften him, making him too passive to
defend himself against real enemies. He can't imagine a world where
he doesn't have to be at the ready at every moment. Of course, this
attitude makes befriending confusion rather difficult. A mad warrior
has no friends.

If there is anything to get used to on this path, it is *repetition of
pattern*. The fall back to habitual ways is a natural part of the journey home. Like turtles, we stick our head out until it becomes too
uncomfortable, and then we retreat to the safety and familiarity of
our shell. The time we spend under the shell can be just what we need
to integrate new experiences into our usual ways of being. So long as
we persist in sticking our head back out a little further each time, we
continue to grow. Three steps forward, two steps back, *is* progress.

As the day progressed, I found myself in the middle of an intense negotiation between the Warrior and Little Missy. The struggle was about my own identity, but I couldn't help feeling like a passenger in the back of a swerving car while others fought for the wheel. The Warrior wanted me to practice law NOW. Little Missy wanted me to postpone the decision to practice until after I did another workshop at Omega—an emotional healing workshop led by Terry Hunt. I had never heard her so adamant: "Something there will rock your world."

By nightfall, an inner compromise was reached. I would do the August workshop and then begin my practice in September. But there was a condition attached. The Warrior insisted that I rent the office before leaving for the workshop. I called my friend with a commitment to rent.

Unbeknownst to me, I was about to live in the question of whether I would practice law or leave it to actively explore other possibilities. I wasn't ready to hold the space for all my confusion at once, but I had apparently gotten close enough for my most pressing questions to wind their way to the surface demanding to be lived. No more waiting at the gate—the next course of action had oddly arisen, and my spirit was stepping through, one baby step at a time....

6 Living in the Question

*When you see a new trail, or a footprint you do
not know, follow it to the point of knowing.*

—SIOUX PROVERB

Sitting with the other participants in the workshop space, I felt
a strong impulse to flee. With ego eyes, I harshly judged everyone in the circle: *Look at these victims. Look at the lines on their faces! How
worn-out these people are!*

Terry arrived and my disdain deepened. As we shared our stories,
he cried about the death of a dear friend. The more he wept, the more
I judged: *A male workshop leader, crying? These people are freaks! I'm a
lawyer—what am I doing here? Get me out of here!*

Terry shared his philosophy. Abuse victims learn that the art of
living is the art of avoiding pain. We survive, but are we alive? In the
workshop we would do various exercises to bring us back into the
world of feeling and to re-introduce us to the pleasure principle.

On the healing journey, many of us devote a lot of our energy to
healing our trauma. Sometimes we are focused on our pain for many
years without experiencing any real pleasure. Sometimes this is absolutely necessary. But when we are ready, we have to remember to invite
pleasure into our daily experience. Good feelings are a manifestation
of our healing, and they are also essential to it. Pleasure nourishes and
strengthens us. This is often missed in the therapeutic movement.

At first, surrendering to the workshop was impossible. I lay in my
tent at night and planned my morning getaway. The last group I had
been deeply vulnerable with was my family, and I had been savaged
when I revealed myself.

I wondered at the complex nature of my resistance. An artful dodger
indeed, my monkey mind jumped from one treetop to another, as far
as possible from the feelings percolating below. At one point, I argued

with Terry, relying on conflict to take me out of my fearfulness. In one partner exercise, we took turns answering the question "How have I hurt you?" I answered but very subtly avoided my partner's gaze. Sometimes we sang corny verses. I mouthed the words, but made my breath shallow so that I couldn't really *feel* them.

I went for a long walk on a dirt road near Omega. Leaving the road, I cut through the forest in the direction of God-knows-what. I sat down at the base of a tree to listen. There were wisdoms rising to the surface of my consciousness: "You need to live your life as an on-going question. This is not a passive process. It is an active exploration of the boundless and eternal mysteries of who you are. Recognize that you created this moment. When a question emerges, live it until it is clarified. Live *in* the heart of inquiry."

That night, I went back to watch Terry work with volunteers. He placed a pile of pillows in the center of the room. Did anyone have anything they needed to release? A very gentle woman walked up to the pile. Without any urging, she went nuts hitting the pillows. Watching her touched into my own well of anger. I couldn't pretend that I was different from these people anymore. We were all plugged into the same electric rage grid.

After everyone left, I set up the pillows again. I smashed them until I was ready to fall over. I went back to my tent and fell asleep. I woke up in the middle of the night crying intensely. This was different than the pain I had touched in my individual therapy. Something about being held in the group embrace excavated our collective grief. I cried for all of us, for most of the night.

When I returned to the workshop the next morning, my ego eyes were closed. Releasing my holdings had opened my heart. As we sang one of Terry's schmaltzy songs, a stranger in the group laid her head on my lap, turning my head toward her so she could look into my eyes. At first I resisted—how could I bare my soul to a perfect stranger? She pulled my head back: *stay here, stay here.* My eyes began to tear. Her eyes, too. Strangers no more, we were quietly crafting a bridge from one soul to the other.

After lunch, we began the Holotropic Breathwork phase of the workshop. Created by Stanislav Grof, this method uses the breath to excavate unconscious emotional holdings and invite non-ordinary states of consciousness. I began as a witness, holding the space for my partner's journey. I helped him with his blindfold and sat down beside him in case he needed anything. He started to breathe deeply, in sync with the loud psychedelic music. Within only a few moments he was flailing his arms and legs about while banging his head against the pillow. After sustaining this rhythm for thirty minutes, he turned himself over onto his stomach and became quite still. Then he began to sob deeply, his body shaking from head to toe.

I looked around the room at the other breathers. Some were screaming louder than the music, some appeared to be having a tantrum or speaking in tongues—God knows what. Others were lying back with blissful smiles on their faces.

I marveled at what I saw. Most of the members of the group were relatively well-adjusted people. Some were highly successful in their fields. If you had met them on the street, you would think that they were as emotionally healthy as the next person. Yet, when granted permission to breathe deeply into their center, their usual manifestations were instantly exposed as false. Like a wave of truthfulness, the breath washed away the lies. How could I ever take the masks we wear seriously again?

Midway through this session, I had an epiphany. While watching a burly man in full-on tantrum, I caught a glimpse of my innate image floating into awareness. It was clear as day. In this lifetime, I was called to help others unmask. I was called to be an Essence worker. I felt chilled as the call rolled around inside me—authenticity chills, the sweet sensations of truth. Although surprised, I knew that I was finally looking in the right direction.

On the soulshaping journey, the choice to expand is often made in some subterranean cavern, out of view of our daily defenses and distractions. It is the nature of our innate image to whittle away in the deep within, invisibly preparing us for change while our conscious mind is somewhere else entirely. By the time our resistance realizes what has happened, we have already been brought one step closer to who we really are. As our path becomes truer, the visible and invisible worlds begin to merge and these processes become more conscious.

I watched the breathers remove their blindfolds and open their eyes. Most were transformed, their faces soft and open. They had momentarily shed their masks and breathed their original face back to life. Now, there's a before-and-after photograph worth taking!

Off to See the Wizard

The next morning, my partner blindfolded me and wished me a good voyage. Where did he think I was going? The psychedelic music began to thump. I couldn't think—that was the idea! At first, I resisted the intense breathing. I saw what had happened to the others.

In due course the breath took over. I could hyperventilate with the best of them. My hands and feet began to tingle. Then I lost feeling in my extremities. My energy started to circulate up and out the top of my head.

I felt pressure against my body, as though I were squeezing through a narrow space. Familiar images floated in and out of consciousness. Then the breath carried me further out. Ushered along a continuum of consciousness, I waved goodbye to familiar landmarks and headed out for mysterious dimensions.

I entered a dark holding area. I stayed here a moment, then crossed into a dimly lit room. By this point I had lost all self-consciousness.

In the center of the room was an old wooden card table. Sitting around it was a group of my dead relatives. My cousin Donny and my uncles Joe and Benny were playing cards. Auntie Gail was watching them. I heard a familiar voice: "So good to see you, little Jeffrey." It was the voice of Auntie Tilly, my favorite aunt. She had died about twenty years before, but I recognized that gruff voice like it was yesterday. She came into view and held me close. She smelled exactly as I remembered. It all felt so completely real.

I sensed a presence close by. I knew who it was. I turned to see my blessed Beela, still wearing his blue shorts and sleeveless white T-shirt. He felt more like an eccentric wizard than the conservative grandpa I remembered. I put my hands on his arms, looked into his wild eyes, and wept tears of joy.

After some time, he whispered to me: "I love you, Pipik. There is more to this dance than you think. I go on. You go on. *This time you give the gift of openness.* I'll help you along." "But how, Beela? Go where?"

He smiled sweetly and vanished.

When my awareness returned to the workshop space, I was startled to find that I had been breathing for more than two hours. I thought it had been thirty minutes. Timeless realms are funny like that. I took off the blindfold and opened my eyes to a world that would never be quite the same. In the presence of the long dead, I had seen the light of eternal life.

I was completely blown away by the power of the breath. Just a few minutes of intense breathing and I had sailed into the mystic. How many other worlds live only a breathwork away, a hundred breathworks away?

I felt gratitude toward Little Missy, my soul's sherpa on the mountain of Essence. She knew exactly what she was doing when she pushed me into this workshop.

But after a few days away from Omega, doubts crept back in. Was I out of my mind at Omega? Did I imagine all that? I had a dream about Eddie Greenspan. In this dream, I had just begun working in his law office. I looked very old. I had a little office in the back where I worked on small cases. I moved through the office like an outsider, ashamed of what had become of me.

The pull to trial law was back in business.

The Presumption of Essence

The law was breathing down my neck. I received many messages from my lawyer friend. He already had work to send my way. Over the next two weeks, I woke up every day with the intention to go in, but my feet kept walking me in a different direction.

I began to feel sad. It felt like that moment in an intimate relationship when you know that your future does not involve your current partner. One night I went to the office when no one was around. I sat at my desk for a long time, imagining myself cast in this role. I felt agitated. I found my way into the law library downstairs—I had always liked reading case law. I read through a series of Supreme Court decisions. My thoughts kept wandering back to the dirt road at Omega—a library of light.

The next morning, I went to a criminal courtroom to try to find my love for trial law. Instead, I saw the courtroom with new eyes. Rather than a forum for justice, I saw a giant hate party predicated on the illusion of separateness.

I watched the judge needlessly belittle the lawyer, the spectators. I watched the accused sitting in the box, cast in the role of the bad guy. Yet I didn't see a bad guy. I saw someone living out his karma, playing an essential part in this survivalist melodrama.

I tried to imagine how this scene would play out in a world not attached to narrow notions of right and wrong. Okay, maybe he did it, maybe he didn't, but what if we let go of our attachment to duality? How might we understand these events through a soulful lens? What soul decisions brought each player to this stage today? Is their role intrinsic to their true-path? Where would they be without each other?

Then I inquired into my own place in this melodrama. Why was *I* in this courtroom at this moment? I imagined myself in the role of the defense lawyer. No sweet stirrings. No spark in my body. Nothing. I certainly believed in the presumption of innocence that Eddie had fought so hard for, but I didn't seem to covet this game anymore. My soul gaze had shifted from the laws of the land to the laws of the universe: *the presumption of Essence.*

I caught another glimpse of my innate image. While looking at the nasty trial judge, I flashed to a scene with him lying on a massage table with my hands on his head. I was inviting him to open his heart and surrender to the spiritual being living below his robes. He was sobbing. I was fully at peace with path.

I was experiencing a *Soul-shadow.* These are reminders of our innate image cast by our soul throughout our lives. I think of them as "peek" experiences—little glimpses into the path that our soul chose before it came back here. These beacons of light shadow us wherever we go, speaking to us across many channels, always calling us home.

Soul-shadows can arise in many forms. Some are apparently external—distant flutes, serendipitous moments, a microscopic breeze. Others are internal—thoughts, interests, waves of resonance, dreamscapes. When we begin to live more essentially, we become more adept at spotting them. What we once experienced as hints and whispers transform into a more direct experience of the pathways within us.

That evening I met the other associates for a beer. They were completely animated about the details of their court day. They loved the stories. They coveted the prizes. I tried to engage, but I couldn't find a way in anymore. It was small sky. I wanted big sky.

I left the bar very upset. I had worked for years to become a criminal lawyer, and now I had lost the passion. Oh Lord, what had I done? Overcome by fear, I went for a long drive. My fear mounted. I suddenly remembered what it was like to live without structure, without money, without hope.

I drove straight back to the office, put some case law on my lap, and held on tight.

Back in the Saddle Again

Next morning, I jumped right in. A woman was accused of violating the terms of her probation by driving too close to her ex-husband's house. I went to the jail to meet her and hear her sad story. A former nurse, she had lost her job because of her addiction to drugs. She had lost her family. She had skin cancer and various other ailments. She had been out of control for a long time.

As I listened, I felt angry at the system. What this woman needed was therapy and a big hug. She needed it for her, and society needed it for its own protection. If she were acquitted, she would just repeat the same behavior. She couldn't help herself. And if convicted, she would repeat the same behavior after being released. Healing was the only bridge that could shift this paradigm.

I went to work on the defense. I put a lot of time into it. It was a minor case but a major laboratory for my own inquiries.

Whenever I bumped into lawyers I had studied with, I marveled at how similar they were to the individuals I had known three years earlier. It was like they were trapped at the same stage of growth that they came in with. I wondered if that would change over time, or if some professions are, by their very nature, too survivalistic to accommodate real change and growth.

It became immediately clear that the heart-opening work I had done would not serve me here. If I stayed vulnerable, I would be eaten alive in the courtroom. There is such a wide gap between the warrior professions and a more subtle way of being. Once you pass a certain point in your evolution, it becomes very difficult to re-adapt.

Despite tremendous progress, the criminal justice system still reflects the harshness that birthed it. Rather than an opportunity for healing, the system operates like a torture chamber, harshly punishing those who have acted out while conditioning the rest of us that we had better contain our wayward impulses or else we will be locked away too. Sadly, the system actually perpetuates the cycle of hate that it seeks to contain.

Justice of a higher order would surely invite a broader notion of social responsibility and a multi-faceted exploration of what really happened. An accused would enter a courtroom that is more interested in the cause of his actions than the action itself. What cultural, psychological, and even archetypal influences played a role? What can we do as a society to heal those involved and to avoid similar occurrences in the future?

Unfortunately, we cannot depend on the lawyers and judges to shift the current paradigm. Although many of them have the right intention, they are restrained by both their warrior conditioning and the competitive nature of the system itself.

Good criminal lawyers are often in court all day, meeting witnesses and new clients in the evening, and devoting some or all of their weekends to trial preparation. With so little time out of the war zone, it is very difficult to self-reflect or to explore other ways of being. Because they are surviving by their wits alone, pleasure gets re-defined as the absence of pressure, a moment's relief from chronic anxiety.

#paradigmshift

Most trial judges are lawyers plucked from the same barbaric battlefield. Without consciousness, many of them end up acting out their unresolved emotional issues in the courtroom. They don't know any better. I remember my first moments in open court as a student and the egoic satisfaction the judge got by asking me a question I could not possibly know the answer to. I stammered and crashed, and the senior lawyers in the room laughed heartily. In an effort to fit in, I laughed right along with them. Vulture culture, indeed.

Before sitting on the bench, it should be mandatory that all judges spend at least three years as clients in a regular psychotherapy practice. This will help to ensure that they can identify their own issues and biases when they deal with courtroom matters. Without knowing themselves, it is very difficult for them to know when their objectivity is in question.

After a month, I was almost ready to call it quits. I saw my future, and I didn't like it. I saw the sleepless nights and the armored musculature. I saw the need to be heavy so I could throw my weight around. I saw myself trapped in the thinking mind, miles from my heart. I saw the illnesses and the medications that would get me back on the battlefield. I saw myself borrowing energy from my future until the account was empty. I saw my body dying before its time.

Then one afternoon, the Warrior suddenly woke up. I felt the old hunger course through my veins. After the trial, I spent a week planning my law practice. I would fight for better living conditions for the accused. I would fight to humanize jails so that prisoners could heal and re-enter society in a healthier state. I planned to put extra energy into my pet peeve, mental health issues. At the heart of this ambition was the idea that many people accused of crimes are emotionally unwell at the time of their actions—more mad than bad. The "insane" act speaks for itself.

The pendulum of true-path swung back. I dreamt that I was in court defending a case with another lawyer. He cross-examined a key witness, but the witness wouldn't give an inch. He sat down disheartened. Then I stood up and cross-examined him. The prosecution's case fell apart. I was momentarily in my glory. As we left the court building, I collapsed on the front steps. I immediately began to hover above my body, as though that unconscious lawyer were someone else entirely. Perhaps he was.

This dream opened the floodgates of inner conflict yet again. Little Missy knew that I was about to commit to the Warrior, and she nagged at me persistently. I began to have dark and wintry imaginings, like something essential was about to die or, worse, prevented from ever coming to life. I fell up the stairs at my office—a *Reichian slip*? The war of words continued....

> **LM:** If law were still your true-path, there would be no dissonance. Your doubts are harbingers of change. Your soul is ready to learn new lessons.

> **W:** Let's make a deal. I will use my warrior skills for the good. I will be an angel's advocate, fighting tooth and nail to humanize the system.

> **LM:** Trust humanity. If that work needs to be done, someone with that calling will do it when the moment is right. Find your real home.

> **W:** I know where my home is. It is in the courtroom.

> **LM:** No, you know where home *was.* Your soul is called to do other work this time. It is important work, literally a matter of life and death—the life and death of the spirit. The world does worse than imprison "criminals." It imprisons souls.

Caught between a rock and a too-soft place, it all felt hopelessly unresolvable.

Dying to an Answer

I felt something pushing up inside me. Somewhere in the deep within, the powers that be decided it was time. No more information gathering. No more avoidance. Shut up and decide.

I booked a week at my favorite inn in the woods. I hiked quickly along the trail, thinking rather than feeling. My mind was still back there, disparaging the legal profession. Ego hounds. Mad warriors.

Who did these lawyers think they were fooling? Pummeling the competition is easy. Shaping your soul, now that's a challenge!

Then I heard Little Missy whisper: "Law is not your enemy. Falsepath is your enemy." And, of course, this was true. How could I possibly know what was real for someone else? Like any profession, law could be a heightened path. It was all about intention. If it was your karma to do it, it was perfect.

One morning, I lay down on the earth, inviting the natural world to support me. After days spent listening to a mad monkey, I felt oddly mindless. I had walked my way back into my body.

I had the feeling that I was being watched. I looked up and not more than eight feet from me was a large moose. It was hunting season, and he was shaking intensely. I could tell by the way he was looking at me that he was asking for help. As I stared back, I felt myself looking through two lenses. One saw the moose as a worthy adversary; the other wanted to hold him safe. We stared quietly into each other's eyes for a long time.

After he left, I stared into the forest for many hours. With the leaves fallen away, I could see far and wide. What a vast and perfect emptiness! Soon, two clear images rose into consciousness. To the left, a torn-up field. Hanging from a tree in the center was a gladiator's outfit, bloodied and worn. To the right, a fertile field of green. Openhearted muses and wood nymphs danced through the long grass and lay in each other's arms. Could it be this simple?

I held both fields of meaning in my imagination at one time and understood. To the left was where my soul had lived. To the right was the next stage in my soul's journey.

I held this moment for a long time … and then fled. I went back to the cabin and fell asleep. I woke in an agitated start. Yet another dark night of the soul, I was too alive to the question to sleep. Little Missy was at an end with my stops and starts. The Warrior was busily cutting transmission lines and digging trenches, readying for battle.

I watched the sun come up through the cottage window. I felt afraid to dissolve. And I felt equally afraid to live. It felt safer to stay lost in translation than to arrive at the trailhead of truth itself.

I put on my clothes and headed for the trail. Negative feelings flooded me—anger at myself for lingering in this confusion for so long, anger at God for giving me such a complicated path to walk, fear of aloneness—who will love me if I walk the path of most resistance? And then guilt about leaving Eddie. How very odd.

I went back to the cottage and turned on the television. The first channel I clicked to was a soap opera where a gritty man was talking to his wife, admitting his desire to quit his job as police chief and teach school. I changed the channel. Oprah was interviewing James Hillman about one of his wonderful soul books. Was the universe conspiring to help me home? Perhaps that which we search for really does search for us too. #whereareyou

A Leap of Fate

I began a long walk around the lake. After many hours, I sat down in a thicket at the water's edge. The lapping of the water softened my edges. All that remained was the real question, rising and falling on the crest of each wave: What is your truth? I was not getting up without an answer.

My mind flashed back to a life riddled with lies. Who cares about living honestly when you're coming from nothing? Without lies and distortions, I would have never survived my family or the marketplace. The lie got me a piece of the pie. Truth-telling seemed like such a luxurious habit.

At the core of my truthlessness was a fundamentally cynical view of the universe. It may have been Albert Einstein who said that the single most important decision we make is deciding if the universe is benevolent or hostile. I saw a freezing cold lake that would mercilessly swallow me up if given the chance. The world was a dangerous place.

If I was going to shift this paradigm, I needed to make a leap of fate into my innate image, wherever he was. A leap of fate is a jump onto the growing edge of our soul. It is completely new territory. It is natural to be afraid.

I wondered if I really had a choice. Below the weight of resistance, another shape was determined to take form. Could it be stopped even if I wanted to stop it? What happens to those of us who retreat from our calls? Do our guides keep at us? Does the soul feel betrayed and turn against us? Does the call fade into oblivion until the next lifetime?

I looked out at the lake, shivering from fright. All of nature was actualizing its true nature, why couldn't I?

I felt the urge to run. I heard the trumpets of guilt, the voices of pragmatism, the Rabbi telling me to take care of my family. I saw the dying, crying lawman lying on the side of the road. Was I on the verge of a breakthrough, a breakdown, a breakdance?

I heard Little Missy coaxing me along, twanging my attunement fork: "Trust your inner knowing." I had angels on my side, but they could only lead me to a new body of water. It was for me to decide whether I would risk drinking from it or turn back to familiar harbors.

I sensed that it was too late to turn back. Like an inner tsunami, my *emerging-sea* of truth had grown too big to be sidestepped. I either let it emerge or suffer the worst fate of all—living a half-life and knowing it! I had to make the leap....

My attention shifted to a beautiful moment at Terry's workshop at Omega. I repeated this memory like a mantra, inviting myself to believe. If Essence has a voice, it is a gentle one. A soft voice came up from my core: "My truth is that the law was just a pit stop. I am called to take my soul in another direction in this lifetime. The law is done for me."

As the words came out of my mouth, truth chills swept through my body, waves of resonance from the deep within. I had spoken my truth, and body and soul sighed with relief.

7 Insight and Opening

Security is mostly a superstition. It does not exist in nature, nor do the children of humans as a whole experience it. Avoiding danger is no safer in the long run than outright exposure. Life is either a daring adventure, or nothing.

—HELEN KELLER

After leaving law I felt lost. Instead of jumping into life, I passively waited around for my next path to appear. I had cleared the space—now where am I already?

After weeks like this, Little Missy got busy with me. Now the wake-up call was alarming me from within whenever I tried to fall asleep. I listened in, as she captured the adventuring spirit that lies at the heart of the soulshaping journey:

A sense of who you are will not unfold if you go to sleep, lazily waiting for life to come to you. Never confuse conscious effortlessness with unconscious laziness. There will be angels and helpers, but they cannot do the work for you. They just remind you of what you already know. The rest is up to you. Finding your way home requires a spirit of adventure. It does not mean that you always have to do. It means that whatever you are doing, or not doing, is experienced as a spiritual inquiry, an information gathering, an active exploration of reality. Sitting still can be a profound adventure if you are present and inquisitive.

Pierce the smokescreen of fearful indifference. Adventure heartily. Have faith in the shaping of what you cannot see.

A Sense of Wander

My first conscious adventure was on the meditation cushion. Although I had meditated occasionally for years, I had never developed a disciplined sitting practice. I always had a hard time sitting still, and I could never quite reconcile the meditative quest for emptiness with my search for true-path. Meditation seemed like the wrong vehicle for my aspirations.

Nevertheless, I began every day with an early morning sitting. While sitting, I yawned almost every time I breathed into held muscles. My back was tight and strained. My left knee screamed when I crossed my legs. My hips were inflexible. Who knew?

I watched as my tireless mind diverted me from my discomfort with meaningless thoughts. I thought about how cool it was that I was meditating. I saw mounds of ice cream floating by. How many times can a person re-think the cost of a new muffler? I was locked in a mind maze with no exit door.

Toward the end of autumn, I gave up on meditation. What seemed like the simplest thing, being present, was seemingly impossible. As a North American urbanite, I couldn't even begin to empty myself of distraction.

I went back to the cabin in the woods. One evening, the inner gate opened again. A little voice whispered in my inner ear, "Go back to school." I knew what it meant: finish my master's degree in psychology and begin a training program in a body-centered psychotherapy.

When I got home, I signed up for the next semester at Saybrook Graduate School, and I applied for the *Bioenergetics* training program to begin the following autumn.

Over time, soul adventuring crystallized into two forms: *Depth Charges* and *Authentications*.

In the context of spiritual path, depth charges are intentional efforts to ignite our inner knowing and excavate our *soul-scriptures* from below the surface of our daily lives. By confining ourselves to a predictable range of experience, we often fail to come into contact with ways of being that might be more fitting to our particular soul's journey. Sometimes we need to drop a depth charge to bring them to the surface. Sometimes we need to turn our world upside down in order to see straight.

At the heart of the depth charge is the quest for the involuntary. I think of it as a sort of self-forgetfulness, where we allow ourselves to let go of our organizing systems and surrender completely to the unknown. In order to self-forget, we have to deal with the clinging ego—no easy feat. This is not about diminishing our self-concept, or undermining us when we most need to feel good about ourselves. It is about humbling our ego when it is too big for its britches, and making it porous enough for a depth charge to get through.

As the next chapters will illustrate, depth charges can take many forms. Some are terrifying free-falls into inner space through breath-work, bodywork, radical changes in diet. Some are outward forays into the scary unknown: terrifying workshops and vision quests, intimate relationships with people who challenge and awaken us, a quest for *trouble*.

Depth charges can also be gentle efforts to vacate our usual ways of being. They might include making love in a different way, dating someone different from our usual pattern, or taking trips to foreign countries with the intention of exploring shifts in perception and self-identification. #Chicago 2017

Authentications are intentional efforts to authenticate those pathways that have called us. When the soulular phone rings, we answer the call by trying the voice on for size. We give it a shot. As we explore it, we check its authenticity against our soul-scriptures: How does this compare? Does it feel like true-path or am I walking down a blind alley?

My next adventure was of a psychic nature. I went to see a psychic named John Pothiah. I had heard extraordinary things about him but remained skeptical. What could he know that I didn't know?

He led me to a little room in his house. He stood in front of me and said something about reading my auras. Then he proceeded to tell me my story. He said I had been handed everything in previous lives. He said I had developed a strong interest in justice over many lifetimes.

I had been a lawyer many times (I had told him *nothing* about me). I had been in camps in Nazi Germany and my dignity had been taken away.

He said that in this lifetime, I was to earn it all myself. I was to study the psychological and mystical and research my self. I was called to write about my inner studies and motivate in the areas of personal growth. I was here to help remove dogma and teach that love is the great religion. I would find my intimate partner "only when you know who you are." My path would come together at age forty-two.

If the best adventures are those that turn our expectations upside down, then I was in a full-blown headstand. This stranger seemed to know my story inside out. Every word he uttered resonated.

This path can feel so lonely. Pothiah reminded me that I was never really alone. Those images of true-path that seemed so privately held were actually seeds planted in the Great Beyond, matters of public knowledge for those who know just where to look. And, most satisfying, I was actually needed for what I brought.

Body Masks

My passion for the quest intensified. I decided to do some therapy sessions with Alexander Lowen, one of the founders of Bioenergetics, a brilliant body-centered psychotherapy. Images of Lowen's face had come to me in dreams for months. What better way to learn how to surrender than with an old warrior of the heart?

I had four profound sessions with him at his home office in Connecticut. He lived in the heart of a horse farm, and there were horses and geese everywhere. While sitting in the waiting room, I would hear the noisy parrot screaming from his perch in the living room. A big dog would stumble in to greet me, yet another reminder of my animal nature.

Eventually the wise old owl himself would appear. Lowen was a little man with eyes vibrant like a wild mustang. A force of nature, this man practiced what he preached. You could just feel it. He would take me into a little room with an uncomfortable little straight-back chair, a beat-up old mattress, and a breathing stool that looked like a primitive stretching device. This room was not set up for floaty-soft, beating-around-the-bush psychotherapy. Like him, it was direct and it was alive. I liked it.

All our sessions began the same way: we talked. All the while, he would stare at my body. He was looking for my real story: How does this man breathe? How tight are his muscles? Where are the energetic blocks? How does he hold himself together? How does he defend against the moment? What do his eyes say?

In Lowen's view, childhood trauma and an overwhelming culture separate us from who we really are. We restrict our breath and tighten our body to defend against difficult feelings and to remain in control. Unfortunately, our self-protection comes at a high price. We have blocked the vibratory flow of energy and frozen the trauma along the mind-body continuum. We have deadened ourselves in order to stay alive.

At the core of Bioenergetic therapy is the idea that mind and body are functionally the same. If we do not make the effort to transform in both dimensions, we will not heal and change.

On the physical level, the client is engaged in a series of exercises that deepen the breath, open contractions and tensions, and excavate the emotional material trapped in the body. The more open and energized the system, the more emotional memory comes to the surface. When emotions emerge, their expression is encouraged in many forms, including crying, shouting, throwing a tantrum, hitting, and kicking.

The mind itself is engaged through a reasoned effort to make sense of one's history and of what is happening on a body level. It is especially important to understand how the personality defenses are mirrored by body defenses: How has this client coped with early trauma? What personality defenses has she developed to protect herself (projection, denial, false sense of superiority, spacey thinking)? How are those defenses reflected in the way that she lives in her body (contraction, armored musculature, head held high, loose pelvis)?

Ideally, the therapy leads to a deeper connection to the present moment. Defensive patterns are replaced with a fluid way of being, a more integrated body-mind, and a stronger energy system better able to handle life stresses. According to Lowen, healthy people experience vibration throughout their entire body and live energized, heartfelt, and thoughtful lives.

In each session, Lowen instructed me to breathe. I would breathe, but he was not persuaded. I breathed in just enough air to survive but not enough to fill me with feeling: shallow breath, shallow life. He likened my situation to driving a car with a flat tire. Air is the cushion that protects the body from stresses. I didn't have enough air in my tires. He would instruct me to breathe deeper: deep breath, deep life. I tried, but there was very little room in me.

Whenever I breathed beyond my usual comfort zone, I dipped into an enormous well of grief held in my chest, reminding me of the still-untapped depths of my own suffering. When I resisted, Lowen would push me: "Breathe, man! Breathe yourself back to life!"

In my eyes he saw tremendous fear, even primal terror. This fear was reflected in the tightness of my body. My muscles were rigidly clamped together. My range of motion was limited. A slave to survival, I was built to move along the path for days on end, without rest or pleasure. I was one downtight guy.

Although Lowen thought that the rigidity was a defense against my overwhelming mother, I wondered if there wasn't more to it than that. What if Mommy was just the scapegoat for the real source? My brothers had not gone warrior in response to her—why not? What if my rigidity originated in my soulshape: warrior soul, warrior body? What if body and soul are functionally the same, in the same way that mind and body are?

After our last session, I was startled at how calm and hopeful I felt. The veils of separateness had fallen away. Opening my body had again opened the gate to Essence. It was becoming crystal-clear that I had to shed my body's habitual answers before I could genuinely explore its essential mysteries.

The same session also shed light on my so-called "absent-mindedness." In reality, I was not absent-minded. I was actually all mind, so lost in some abstract area of thought or worry that I was unaware of anything outside of it. This is why I often forgot where I had parked my car. I wasn't really *there* when I parked it. I was *absent-bodied.*

Throwing Momma from the Brain

I went home and did one hour of Bioenergetics every morning, but after a few weeks I began to neglect it. It was still very difficult to integrate new ways of being into my home life.

In search of deeper pastures, I signed up for an eight-day retreat with Jack Kornfield and Stanislav Grof called "Insight and Opening," a combination of Insight Meditation (vipassana) and Holotropic Breathwork.

On the first morning, Kornfield invited us to meditate. I looked around the room and saw members of the group through a bioenergetic lens. I saw armored bodies, trapped vitality, unexpressed sadness and anger. I saw people trying to shift out of their bodies into the safe haven of the mind. Was this meditation, or medication?

With Lowen, I had entered a meditative state only after energizing my body and releasing emotional holdings. Could it happen any other way? Can we really be in the moment if the physical and emotional bodies are tied in knots? Shouldn't we empty the vessel first?

I stopped judging and tried to meditate. Of course, I couldn't turn off my own monkey mind: endless past regrets, tireless future-tripping.

I imagine the monkey mind in almost militant form. Boxcar after boxcar of helmeted monkey soldiers stop at our station. They all have the same agenda: to distract us from settling into the moment. Although they would appear to be an enemy of the sacred, this is not really the case. Sentries at the gate to survival, this army of distraction developed to protect us. Focusing on a single point of awareness has been too dangerous for humankind with food to gather, enemies to watch for, perils everywhere.

Unfortunately, the soldier monkey outlives its usefulness. Long after dangers have passed, he still jumps onto our mental screen and distracts us from reality.

On the second morning of this workshop, I touched into my own unexpressed sadness and anger. Now I understood—it was actually me who was the sitting time bomb. Not everyone needed to move their body before they could sit and meditate. I did.

The next day I had my chance. It was the first of two Holotropic Breathwork sessions. I put on my blindfold and intensified my breath. After some time, my inner world felt weightless. I saw a cavern and I entered it. There was a fire up ahead, a fire of essential light. I walked toward it and sat down. Across from me appeared a man. He looked just like me, except his eyes were peaceful. I reached through the fire to touch his hands. We stayed like this for a moment. He felt so familiar.

Then I looked away, hungry for diversion. I wasn't used to being so alive to myself. I shallowed my breath and fell back to Mother Earth as I knew it. I lay with my eyes blindfolded for a long time, inwardly berating myself. Why couldn't I stay in the fire longer?

Before the final breathwork, I asked Dr. Grof what to do when I stopped myself from going deeper. He said to keep coming back to the intense breathing: "The breath will see you through." I lay down on the mat blindfolded. The music began. I started to breathe strongly. Then I sensed that I was about to cross over into somewhere scary-intense. I stopped breathing. I wanted to hide.

I made my choice and came back to the breath. My hands and feet started to tingle and my energy began moving into the core. Then everything went quiet.

I entered a realm that I can only describe as Forgiveness. I sensed the presence of my sister's spirit. She had died when she was only a few days old, and I had always felt responsible for her death. I could feel her spirit assuring me that I was not to blame. Everything was okay. Then I encountered my first love and hugged her. We took hands and went into another realm and apologized to a fetus we had aborted when we were young.

Somewhere below my hunger for forgiveness was a wellspring of anger. I turned onto my stomach and began to punch the mat with tremendous ferocity.

I saw an image of my mother standing near the head of my bed telling me that I was bad. I heard her shrill voice cutting through me, imprinting her shaming mantra on my cells. Then my hitting blossomed into a full-body tantrum, breath and limbs moving together in an oddly choreographed dance of hate and liberation. Meditation in motion.

I felt her physical form on my back, holding me down. I asked my helper to get the assistants to try to pin me. I wanted to simulate a lifetime of being pinned down by the belief that I was not good enough. I wanted to push against her judgment and disdain. Two trainers came and lay over my back. They tried to pin me down, but I would throw them off each time. How strong is the body when it is speaking its truth!

I stayed with this power surge longer, reaching an even deeper wellspring of frustration. It was not just my self-concept that was hungering for liberation. My soul was also tired of being buried below a bushel of shame.

I was awestruck by the depths of my shame, by the mother-load that obstructed my path. I had lugged this body around for thirty-five years without fully knowing, and the world seemed to reward me for not knowing. The more effectively I wore my masks, the better I was rewarded by a culture that celebrated the outer life. It was like a giant conspiracy to avoid emotional truth.

With the weight of my shame shackles, it is little wonder that I couldn't stay connected for very long before falling back into separateness. Birthed in shame, the bad boy's sentence was to stumble through the cosmos alone, forever prohibited from connecting to anything outside himself. A separate universe felt safer, and the limits of my isolated entitlement.

I walked down the road and sat on the ground beside a giant field of bulrushes. I marveled at the difference in my perception. Before the breathwork, separate me had looked out at a million bulrushes. Now the field of bulrushes was a metaphor for a boundless field of unified perception. Again, open the body and a new true universe unfolds.

I got up from the bulrushes to walk back. I had opened the gate to Essence yet again. Now what? What comes after the clearing?

Ascending with Both Cheeks on the Ground

When I sat down to meditate that evening, I felt like a different person from the one who had last sat on this cushion. Few disruptions to clarity, little agitation, easy breath. The monkey mind was fast asleep.

The first thing I noticed was the emptiness. I felt emptied of localized pushes and pulls, cries for attention, self-distractions. At first the emptiness bored me. I had nothing to think about, nothing to worry about. I was so used to the monkey mind that I didn't know how to be without him. His chatter had become my idea of fullness.

I stayed with the emptiness and it began to reveal itself differently. After two hours on the cushion, visions flooded my consciousness. I was in the midst of a windstorm. I was in the heart of a mountain. I was floating through space. These images were not from beyond, they were realities held within. I was always the Plains of Abraham, the salmon swimming upstream, the lover's spat at Fisherman's Wharf. I was always you reading me.

As I entered this more unified consciousness, I saw that the emptiness is not empty at all. It is actually quite full and engaging. In the heart of true emptiness is a magically interwoven landscape filled with essential riches.

I had entered the Essential realms. This world is no mythical construct—it is the world as it really is.* In this dimension, basic needs are not shelter and food but creativity and intimacy, and the only real crimes are moments spent away from it. We call it extraordinary because we settle for less than what truly calls us. We think it vast because we choose to live so small. *

The gates opened wider. I saw myself in the heart of the Everything, a portrait of true self hanging in a gallery of light. At first *Soul-traces*— images of soul history—whispered in and out of consciousness. I saw a black man glistening with sweat on a bloody battlefield. I saw a sad little girl walking into a bleak cottage somewhere lush. I saw myself eating a popsicle on Clayhall Avenue in Toronto thirty years ago. Rumi understood,

As essence turns to ocean
the particles glisten
Watch how in this candleflame instant blaze
all the moments you have lived.

Then other images rose into consciousness, images of true-path. Fingers of light were reaching through the Everything to point me home. Fears swirled through my body. I suddenly felt afraid to die.

I stayed with my breath, my best friend, my truth-teller. Up from the depths came the mantra "Give over, give over.... " Dark imaginings be damned, it was time to surrender. Somewhere in Buddhaland was a ray of sunshine with my name on it. I hungered to feel it on my face. I wanted the light. I stayed with the unfolding.

In the wee hours of the morning, I gave over. I saw the man I had fled at the fire of essential light float back into consciousness. He still looked exactly like me, but he *felt* different. He was vital and surrendered, hearty heart heart.

I stayed with this image and it morphed. I saw him sitting under a tree with pen in hand. I saw him holding someone's head in silence. I saw him staring into a lover's eyes, soul-gazing. I was soul-gazing, too.

I didn't know this guy, but I knew him so very well. I was reading directly from my soul-scriptures. I was one lens closer to the truth. I stared into his eyes, I stared into my eyes, the who I am of this moment eyeballing the who I might be in the next.

I got up from the cushion at 5 a.m. What a night. A rare bright night of the soul. Insight meditation, indeed!

Actualizing My Soul-Scriptures

Until now, I had imagined that finding myself was only about identifying my career direction. Yet as I watched my innate image sitting peacefully by the fire, I realized that the heart of the matter was archetypal transformation, the way of being that I needed to embody in this lifetime. Like one who runs to a career counselor while ignoring the deeper questions of soul identity, I had been looking in the wrong direction.

That way of being was surrender. Images had emerged of how I might manifest this in the world, but these tasks were meaningless if I didn't embody the way of being at the source. Becoming a more surrendered being was the work that I was here to do, and it would necessarily permeate everything—my career, my relationships, my way of relating to the moment itself.

To this point, I had conceived of soulshaping as the process of distinguishing my real self from my adaptations and disguises. All I had to do was knock down the wall, and I would find my intact soulshape waiting for me.

As I stared into the eyes of my innate image, I recognized the error of this assumption as well. There was actually no intact soulshape waiting to be discovered. There was, instead, a soulshape waiting to be formed. The hearty fire man was merely my innate potentiality, a vision of the possible. He was the direction home, but it was not a *fait accompli*. The key to my soul's transformation was the efforts I made to form the new shape with my own two hands. This is the essence of soulshaping. Not free will or determinism, but free will *and* determinism. You uncover the innate image, and then you do the work to embody it.

It felt like far more free will than I had bargained for. Although it felt empowering to be my own shaper, it also represented a whole new level of responsibility, a crossover into adulthood—into godhood? Was I up to the task?

8 Love's Lessons

*Eternity waits behind the transparent door of
each moment. Love the beloved, and that door
swings open: Eternity enters, pouring the wine
no one who drinks can ever recover from.*

—RUMI

I came home and worked at surrender. An odd thing, to work at
surrender.

I began to sleep on my back, with my heart open and vulnerable.
I listened to New Age music on perpetual repeat. I hung backwards
over a breathing stool. I invited my massage therapist to peel away
more of my warrior armor.

But my explorations soon faded. I was stuck in downtown Toronto,
writing papers for graduate school and operating a growing business.
I watched myself go back into Warrior as a way of being.

I returned to the country to soften my edges. While I was lying by
my favorite brook, the gate to Essence opened. It was as it always was,
except that this time what had passed for profound openness now felt
even a bit closed. Before, a brief moment of surrender was a giant leap
in presence. But I had opened deeply at the Insight Meditation. I was
ready to go further in.

I turned on the soulular phone and asked the universe to help me
open my heart: "Please help me. Please open me. Please bring me
love. Please.... "

The universe began bumping me into people whom I had parted
from at points of tension, significant relationships whose remnants
weighed heavily on my heart.

The first relationship was with Marcus, an old friend from high
school. I had been involved in helping to get his brother out of jail.
Afterwards, I carried unexpressed anger toward him. One afternoon

I finally admitted the depths of my anger to myself. That very night I bumped into Marcos for the first time in years.

I focused a therapy session on my remaining anger. After the session, I rode my bike onto the next street. Marcos almost walked right into me as he crossed the street. I said what I had to say. I felt my heart-load lighten.

The next morning I bumped into a friend of my old girlfriend Robin at a neighborhood restaurant. It was an instant reminder of unresolved issues. That afternoon I went for a shiatsu with a new practitioner, Michael Matheson, who said that I was holding some unresolved feelings in one of my legs. As he worked the area intensely, memories of long-buried conflicts with Robin rose into awareness. That afternoon I went to the library to study and Robin walked by. I hadn't seen her in nearly two years.

The next day I went for a lunchtime walk with a friend and an odd feeling came over me. When we turned the last corner, I saw Robin walking into a store just ahead of us. Connecting the sacred dots, I tapped on the window to say hello. She turned and smiled. We stood there, on opposite sides of the glass, warmly staring at one another. Her eyes were forgiving. It was lovely. I hadn't realized how much I needed that. The shame knot loosened a little bit more.

My intuition told me that I was no accidental tourist in these encounters. It felt like something was opening, something in the energy of things. The universe was getting busy with me.

Prep School

In early June I went to see Lowen again. We did deeper work around the holdings in my body. I wanted to believe that the source was the culture, as always, but he led me down a different path. He kept asking: What are you holding against?

He handed me a red towel and told me to twist it: "Get into the hate, Jeff. Kill your mother." It felt intuitively right, but I resisted. He kept at me. He said I was living falsely. Neurotics numb their feelings; healthy people live in them.

I trusted this man, so I began to twist his red towel. The first thing I felt was fear of getting into trouble—could she hear me back there in Canada? I remembered pushing her away from me as a little boy. As she fell back on the bed, a little voice came out of my mouth: "Mommy." How confusing. Hate and love sadly interwoven. If you love the hateful mother, you hate yourself. If you own the hate, you have to face the painful fact that you are not loved.

I kept twisting and crossed into hate. Once the door opened, it wouldn't stop. I let the twisted sounds of congealed rage come out of my mouth. *Murderous rage.* I screamed "Shut up!" over and over: "Shut up or I'll kill you!" Was this her neck? Don't judge, just twist. I could see her face, feel her presence: "You tormented me! I hate you!"

I left Lowen's office in a spent stupor. On the long train ride back, I began to integrate. It was only one session, but it was pattern-shattering. For perhaps the first time, I knew that I could take care of myself without having to close my heart.

Simultaneously I experienced a rare softening toward my mother. Was that forgiveness trickling through my heart? How hard I had tried to forgive her through years of psychotherapy! Now I got it—that was all premature forgiveness. I couldn't actually forgive her because I hadn't honored the depths of my anger first.

In a survivalist world, we are often encouraged to "forgive and forget" before our anger interferes with our capacity to put food on the table. New Age and psychological communities also harp on the importance of forgiveness. It has become a mantra of emotional health and heightened consciousness. Of course, forgiveness is a beautiful thing, but it is essential that it arise organically. Many of us claim to have forgiven while still holding toxic emotions below the surface: *the forgiveness bypass.* The truth is that we cannot will ourselves into forgiveness. If we try to forgive before we have moved the feelings, inauthenticity blocks our path. We cannot be in the real, because we are not emotionally real. Our cells are still back there.

In property law, the law of adverse possession allows us to become the owner of someone else's property if we use it for a certain length of time. Emotional property is no different. When someone takes their stuff out on us, it moves from them to us. It remains ours unless we choose to give it back, to express rather than repress the feelings that arise from the experience(s). The longer we hold on to it, the more likely it is that their property will concretize inside us and become fully our own: *the law of averse possession*. Often without realizing it, we move through our life emotionally taxed for carrying someone else's stuff. By not saying "f*#k you," we have f*#ked ourselves.

Best to not buy into the cultural judgment around anger—it is *not* an unworthy emotion. If it is expressed in a healthy way, it will restore our emotional integrity and bring us back to life.

After Lowen, I felt optimistic. I had the oddest sense that something was about to happen that would profoundly change my life. I began to have recurring dreams about a red-haired woman, sensations of deep abiding love.

I had signed up to attend the first conference of the United States Association for Body-Centered Psychotherapy. In choosing the post-conference workshop I would attend, I spent days debating between the *Core Energetics* founder, John Pierrakos, and Ron Kurtz, founder of the *Hakomi* method. I would choose one, cross his name out, and then pencil in the other. I finally chose Kurtz without knowing why. I knew almost nothing about him.

Before I left for the psychology conference in Boulder, I told people I was going to meet a great love there.

While waiting for the plane at the Toronto airport, my shiatsu therapist Michael Matheson showed up. He was taking the same plane! He had decided at the last minute to come to the conference. I had the strangest feeling that he was somehow linked to whatever would follow.

The Magical Mystery Tour (Step Right UP)

At the conference something sweet was circling around, within me. A woman would get on the elevator and I would look at her, wondering, Are you the one?

I spent time with an old friend and wondered: *Is it you? It doesn't feel like it, but if we spend a little more time together, maybe we can craft a soul connection.* We all know that game.

I caught a glimpse of a red-haired woman standing in the center of the lobby. There was something about her. Then she was gone. Frustration. Next day, same lobby, she looked at me directly: *Where have you been, smiling eyes? You are so familiar to me.*

Two days later I attended the Ron Kurtz post-conference workshop. We all sat in a circle. The door opened and there she was. Beautiful being sat down facing me. Our eyes met and I felt my soul rising up to meet its other half. All heaven broke loose. The world around us fell away. We stayed with our eyes locked for minutes, deepening into pools of timeless knowing. Who am I looking at? Are these two souls or one?

Her name was Rachel. Dinner break, I asked her to join me. She thought it was silly that I needed to ask. We sat down by the river. I was overwhelmed by our shared nature. We discovered the same music, moved through the same phases, experienced similar suffering. We loved the same Rumi poems (always a good sign). We had the same picture on a wall in our bedrooms.

We walked to the hotel arms touching. There was no question, I had felt this being against me before. I didn't have to ask her—she felt it too. We knew each other from time immemorial. What happened two hundred years ago? Did I not tell you to turn right at the enchanted forest? Why did you go left?

The next day we went on a day trip. In her presence, the psychic locomotive slowed to a crawl. The petty details fell away, the essentials emerged. I felt profound love sensations coursing through me, stroking my heart back to life. She was a mouthful, a handful, a dram of sweet metaphors. I already loved her completely.

We arrived at Eldorado Canyon. My armor peeled back. Who needs armor when you have magic? She coaxed me to run with her. I suddenly felt overwhelmed and afraid. Ground yourself, Jeffrey, this is way out there!

We stopped at a big rock beside the cold river. We stood on it and kissed. The rock became an eternal bridge, erected for us and us alone, crossing us deeper into wonder with every kiss. I was calmed and mesmerized at the same time. As we kissed, my breath deepened. I needed deep breath to feel *all* of this. Soon my breath relaxed. We breathed in unison. The breath of the fluid universe came to join us. We all breathed as one.

Not ten minutes after leaving the rock, we stumbled into Michael Matheson walking up the path. What are the odds? Interestingly, he told us that he had just become involved with the woman that Rachel was staying with. This was the same woman who had told her about this conference when they met in Florida. What are the odds?

Rachel and I spent the night together. Whatever resistance I had known to focusing on a woman's pleasure fell away. The smell of her body comforted and ignited me, heaven scent. My usually selfish hands became tools of devotion, praying at the temple of her. My fingertips became highly charged love lights, hungrily searching for dark, hidden wonders to infuse with light. For the moment, the Warrior was nowhere to be found.

AscenDance

We met in Pennsylvania a few weeks later. We made love the first night, but I was disconnected. What did I know about soul-gazing? The warrior's version of sexuality was physicality and release.

As we moved through our days, we continued to deepen our recognition of one another. We were together for the first time in this lifetime, and yet we both knew that this moment would come all along. We shared a quiet sense of each other that transcended language. In looking at each other, we stared at our own reflection. Whatever the manifest differences, they were transient, temporal. At the place of Essence, no difference.

We began to fight. Silly things. We didn't fight because we didn't love one another. We were miles from the ungrounded flight of fancy, the romantic illusion between two people who don't really see each other. We were in the heart of Essence, and in this profound vulnerability we were confronted with its opposite. In this pure place, every painful association with vulnerability jumped up before us.

We slept on a mountain. In the morning we sat on its edge and welcomed the day. The valley felt crisper and more infinite with Rachel beside me. She sat naked on a nearby rock. I longed to touch her, but there was no need—I was already touching her. We sat in silence, satiated by each other's divinity.

It was so surprising to me that those annoying habits that drove me crazy in others were completely lovable with someone I had deep soul business with. With Rachel, they were like little splashes in a vast ocean.

Driving home, I felt like an escorted soul, in the safe hands of providence. A moment here was enough to transform consciousness forever. I looked to my left and noticed a beautiful field of pink flowers between the two lanes. It was here to show me, in vivid color, the universe of perception waiting on the other side of perfect love. I would never have noticed it in my usual here now. *Immaculate perception.*

Back home, I became cynical about the connection. For two days I didn't call her. I wondered if I had been seduced by a mad woman. Our connection beckoned me toward a formlessness that was as terrifying as it was compelling.

When finally we talked on the phone, the Warrior dropped to his knees. He had met his match. That afternoon I received a Rumi poem in the mail from Rachel. Perfect timing:

> Don't turn from the delight that is so close at hand!
> Don't find some lame excuse to leave our gathering.
> You were a lonely grape and now you are sweet wine.
> There is no use in trying to become a grape again.

We continued to talk often, and I opened to this delightful feeling of relief. I didn't realize how alone I was, until I wasn't. It is such a relief when great love comes your way after so many years without it. Such a different universe. This love confirmed that I would rather have five minutes of soul love and a lifetime alone, than partner for fifty years with something less. Commitment in the absence of soul connection is just a business deal.

With relief came a sense of vindication. When confronted with the usual commitment request from my girlfriends, I had invariably recoiled. Now I understood why. I had preparatory commitments to honor: clearing the emotional debris that interfered with my capacity to partner, building the internal girders required to sustain a genuine commitment. Before I could really take someone inside, I had to carve a space for her, a canyon for her river of love to run through.

In truth, I had always intuited that a wondrous love connection was waiting in the (angel's) wings. I felt it there, tugging at my soul sleeve, and knew that it would only come my way if I readied myself.

A good friend was always going on about the merits of practical love. For her it was quite simple—make a list of values and personality traits and marry the first person that checks off. Assembly-line love. But the pragmatists don't realize what fifty years in the same room can feel like, particularly if there is no soul bridge between the two people.

What happens if one partner begins to grumble for a more spiritual life? Will they be held back by the practical partnership they committed to seven years earlier? Do they adapt to the lowest common denominator and vibrate at the level of the least growth-full partner? Do they feign commonality at the expense of their clarity? Or do they walk away with three screaming children?

Earlier in the year, I had gone on the Internet and searched through the sites of dozens of retreat centers to consider for a summer visit. Three resonated, all in California—Mt. Madonna Center, Harbin Hot Springs, and Esalen. As it turns out, Rachel was going to Mt. Madonna for a yoga teacher training, and then to Harbin for a vacation. Imagine that!

I met her at Mt. Madonna. We took the Essence elevator up another level as the boundary between us further disintegrated. Initially alone, then co-independent, now soul united, we walked through the mountain garden like one vital being, one ecstatic soul-heart actualizing its soul-scriptures with every beat. In this unity there was no need to say "I love you" as though we were somehow separate. "IU" said it all.

As we continued to dance together, our experience of love blossomed outward. Rumi wonders, "Love so vast, love the sky cannot contain. How does all this fit within my heart?" The answer is that it doesn't. It spills over. As we wandered hand in hand, there was no distinction between us, trees, scents, the hiker ambling by. The forest laughed. We were the laughing forest. Intertwined branches rooted in God. *Tat twam asi.* IU, I-everything.

At the same time, I was sexually reluctant. I could touch her forever, but when it came to intercourse, I couldn't seem to bring heart and genitals together. I was afraid of something on the other side.

One night I almost got there. We were fooling around in the tent and I got excited. It felt like the first time that love itself had ignited my sexuality. After a few moments, I lost my sexual charge. My Warrior knew that this heart sex was the ultimate form of surrender, and he needed to stay in control. Of course, after shutting me down, he beat me up for being inadequate. Just can't please that guy.

Root Awakening

We left Mt. Madonna in a state of conflict and drove to Harbin, arriving in time for the evening chant. A giant wild-looking man sat at the head of the room plucking something called an ektara. His name: Bhagavan Das. I had the strange feeling that I had known him before or that I was destined to know him one day.

He began to chant. The room filled with powerhouse energy. This guy was Mr. Depth Charge. I was both frightened and encouraged by his energy. He was shaking loose and opening wide and he wasn't dying. Maybe I wouldn't?

As I chanted, I felt a strong vibration moving through me. I felt more space opening up inside. The vibration was cracking my armor from the inside out. Afterwards Rachel went to the pools while I went back to the room. As I lay on the bed, I felt that pressure building inside me when the soul is wanting to expand. I also felt its opposite, the fearful small-self expert at sabotage, clinging to what it knows. I lay back and awakened my mantra: Give over, Give over, Get lost! Useless. Too self-conscious. I left my hiding place and went to the pool, where I submerged in the water. This place was like nowhere I had been. The floral scents, the silence, the water, the energy. Harbin is other-worldly, mighty high.

Rachel leaned toward me. We gazed into each other's eyes for a long time. My mind tap turned off. I opened wider. Our love was a truth serum that had to be drunk. Tears began to fall. I felt myself slowly submitting.

We went back to the room and lay down. I felt my soul yearning to merge with her, stretching at its seams. The yearning first took root in my heart—a heart-on of epic proportions—and then spilled over to my genitals. I surrendered to a sexuality that was different than anything before. Love was the sexual turn-on, at last! My usual love-making had no place here. Soul love had its own way of moving me. Lost in a wild free-fall, I experienced a beautifully bareable lightness of being.

We moved together until there was no felt distinction between our bodies. Her pleasure was my pleasure, my arms hers, her breasts mine. We became one unified body-being, crossing the gender bridge with every breath. I was touching she who was me who was God. This was *our* body. We made love many times that night, and each time the soulfire ignited the heartfire ignited the genitals. A wake-down call of the highest order. God is a dish best served juicy.

Afterwards we lay startled, awe-struck. We could only say "perfect" because it truly was. It was wordless, but it said everything perfectly. Holding Rachel's hand was like holding God in the palm of my hand. It was as close to source as I could ever imagine, an irresistible surrender to the love-struck wellspring that sources the *all*. In each other's arms, we could not help but perfect the art at the heart of seamless presence. Even if we wanted to move, where would we go? We were already everywhere. We were already poetry in motion. It was as true a thing as I could ever imagine.

Marveling

Rachel left to take a soak. I lay there, marveling at what was happening to me on this greatest of adventures. In surrendering to this love, my soul had added new ways of receiving and transmitting information. The transformation was manifest throughout my body. There was a liquidity to it, a surrender to what is. My warrior armor had been stripped bare.

Most startling was the quietness of my mind. Love had put my big brain to sleep and revealed its true purpose as servant to the great master, the love-oxygenated heart. This heart-felt universe of perception is where one really *lives*.

I marveled at the genderless nature of soul love. Together, our energies had bridged us into something higher, more whole, holier. Although it was sexual union that took us there, the chemistry was not gender-sourced, nor was the state we entered gender-identified. What got us there was the merging of our twin souls along the heart-genital highway. These longing souls didn't care about body parts. They just wanted to join their other half.

I marveled at the power of relationship to transform consciousness. Like so many men on this planet, I had been too over-identified as an individualist to take my connection to others deep inside. I thought of lonely men everywhere, talking to anyone but not talking about anything real, so desperate for human contact but too heart-severed to actually create it. Love is the antidote for what ails them.

For the first time in my life, I felt absolutely sure why I was here. I was here to love and marry this woman. When the time was right, our love would spill over into the creation of new life. Little souls would be born. It just had to be.

Dark Night of the Soul-Mate

That day, Rachel turned on me. She was scared, but too scared to admit it. The profound vulnerability had awakened old betrayals and she was looking for proof that I would betray her too. Her cross-examination continued for a long time. We left Harbin in a heartbroken huff.

At the airport we found that we were on the same plane to Detroit. We landed in Detroit and raced to watch the sun go down. The loudspeaker announced a gate change. Rachel's plane had been moved to my terminal, to the gate right beside mine. Someone, somewhere, wanted us to hold each other close just a little while longer.

Two weeks later, I went to visit her family home in Louisiana. From the moment I arrived, I knew I was actualizing a soul-scripture written before I was born. The house, those dogs, that walk up the paved road to the dirt road up high, were all part of the blueprint.

We spent half our time loving, half our time fighting. The shadows were circling close. Rachel walked softly but carried a big *shtick*. She became judgmental and mean-spirited. If this had been an ordinary love, I would have been out of there at the first sign of nasty. But I had been brought to my knees by this mesmerizing love experience, and it felt sacrilegious to armor up.

Our conflicts often seemed to emanate directly from our souls—two warrior souls, longing for and resisting their merger in equal measure. At other times I was sure that the pain of the collective unconscious was rising up to obstruct us. We felt our connection to the universe in the ecstasy, why not in the suffering too? Can anyone hold this degree of love safe before the collective unconscious itself has healed?

I returned to Louisiana a week later and asked Rachel to marry me. She said yes. She came to Toronto and we fought like banshees the first night. We fought all night and then woke up the next morning and made perfect love. We were getting used to this dance: open, retreat to defenses, surrender yet again.

We went to a park and I formally proposed. She accepted the ring. Late that evening I felt a sudden need to go for a walk in Wychwood Park, a private community near my home. We left the house and walked Wychwood. As we made the last turn, somebody called my name. We turned around and Michael Matheson stepped out from behind a tree. We almost fell to the ground. How many times had we said his name—"our guardian angel Michael Matheson"—and wondered when he would next appear? Now here he was, on the night of our formal engagement, appearing from behind a tree in a city of millions, a hundred miles from his own home. Rachel and I walked shakily out of Wychwood and sat down on the curb to gather ourselves.

The next month, I went back to see her in Louisiana. Rachel threw the ring at me because I hadn't told my ex-girlfriend that I was now engaged. The issue wasn't the issue. The *fear* was the issue. I went back home and we fought on the phone. I continued to stay open, holding to the gift. Providence supported me in this. Our special songs blared from the radio. There were timely Louisiana license plates and the feathers that appeared at my feet when I went for walks. A few landed in my hair. We were all about feathers.

Rachel moved to Toronto. We went to the Humane Society to get a kitten. We debated her name: Sophie, or Moonlight? We stepped into a shop. The shop owner called to her dog, "Sophie." What kind of madness is this?

The first month was lovely. Our private language burst at the seams. We made a lot of beautiful love at God's banquet table.

Sadly, our little glimpse of heaven was soon interrupted. An old soul with a young psyche, Rachel could only stay close for so long before feeling imprisoned. My psyche was not much older. When she would push me away, it would trigger my JAB and I would try, feverishly, to pull her toward me. Then she would dig in her heels even more. We were unconsciously re-enacting what we lived as children, a power struggle between a woman afraid of her scary father and a man afraid to be abandoned by his mother. Twin Blames.

That winter, there was a horrible snowstorm in Toronto. The mayor called the army out to help. He should have sent them to our house. Souls in anguish, we created the monsters we most feared, one projection at a time.

I went down on my knees countless times and asked God, "Why?" All this serendipity, but for what? We had been gifted something so wondrous, yet we couldn't hold it safe alone. In uncharted territory, with no elders to guide us, in a culture more concerned with ego than Essence, we were adrift alone on this raucous river. Our ship was riddled with holes from our pasts, everyone's pasts, and we had no idea how to patch them. Worse still, we mistook each other for the pirate ship itself. How to stay afloat and ride this hol(e)y ship?

Rachel left for Oakland to do graduate work. The conflicts continued. I fused. She refused. She was on the run, and I refused to stop chasing. She had me by the jabacles, what to do?

One spring night I had a vivid nightmare. I dreamed of my grandfather. He was driving a car through the country. I rode beside him. I told him that Rachel and I intended to move to the country. He gave me an odd look and said, "Sometimes living in the country isn't all it's cracked up to be." Then it got snowy on the road and became difficult to see. Because he was nearly blind, I told him I would drive. He looked at me and said with conviction, "*I* will be doing the driving for a while."

I woke up in a start. I called Rachel before lunchtime, and her exboyfriend answered the phone. It was real early California time. I knew what had happened. I hung up the phone and vomited. I stopped at a pay phone and called back. She answered. I asked her to tell me the truth. She did.

There are no words for that fall from grace. No words.

9 Grumbling Toward Ecstasy

*Restlessness and discontent are the
first necessities of progress.*

—Thomas Edison

Miles to Go Before I Weep

I was soulbroken. I went home and paced. My friend brought me
some alcohol. It took me further into the anguish. With more
triggers than a firing range, I lay on my couch for weeks in the most
intense pain I had ever experienced.

Instead of turning the question inward (why did *I* bring this to
me?), I externalized it. I demanded answers from God: Why make me
whole and rip me to shreds? Why this dirty trick? Why did *you* do
this to *me*?

I felt like a total fool. I had been so sure of us, and so dismissive
of other connections. Meanwhile people in more "practical" relationships were falling asleep together night after night, and I was lying
alone on my couch, with Sophie cat at my side.

I continued looking for an explanation outside myself. I went to
California for a graduate school conference. I gravitated to a workshop
taught by Dr. Jeanne Achterberg, the author of *Imagery and Disease*.
The workshop was focused on a rare kind of soul relationship—Uncommon Bonds. Interesting.

I was blown away by Achterberg's framework. It spoke to every
aspect of my connection with Rachel: the soul's familiarity, the serendipity, the ecstasy and the agony, the transpersonal energy, the sigh of
relief as if coming home after decades of wandering. It was us!

After the course, I went for a long walk in the cool night breeze. I
felt a rare optimism. Maybe we were doing exactly what Providence
intended: opening, retreating and consolidating growth, expanding
outward yet again. I woke in the night with the decision to write my

master's thesis about our uncommon bond. If nothing else, the adventure deserved to be reported.

Then I got a voicemail from Rachel. In a child-like voice, she said, "I can't do it, Jeffrey. I'm too afraid. I'm so sorry. This is just too hard." Then her voice changed and I heard a stranger, armored and aloof.

A new possibility arose. I had seen Rachel as a "runner," someone who flees relationship at the first sign of trouble. But what if Rachel did all the work that she came to do with me? What if our mutual soul-scripture had already been honored?

I couldn't bear this possibility, so I went for numb, the usual program: the couch, mindless videos, heavy food to block my feelings. Soon I couldn't feel a damn thing.

Leggo My Ego

The outer world began to call me. I was paying precious money for an expensive master's program and writing very few papers. I had a stockpile of unread material from the Bioenergetics training program. And my economic comfort zone had segued into debt.

I threw myself back into the world of doing. As any workaholic knows, the trick is to leave little time between projects. That way feelings don't have room to surface. I dedicated the morning to my studies and the rest of the day to making money.

When I finished my coursework, my master's thesis poured out of me seamlessly, its connection to true-path revealed through the clarity and pace of its creation. I finished a hundred-plus pages in thirty-one hours. There was no need for a second draft. Soul-scriptures don't take much editing.

I went to a Bioenergetics conference in Quebec and did a workshop with Frank Hladky, a sturdy therapist who had been working with Alexander Lowen for many years. There, for the first time since I met her, I got into my rage toward Rachel. As I went deeper, I began to touch the grief below. Every time I touched it, I jumped back into anger. By staying angry, I didn't have to surrender to my heartbreak, didn't have to cry. I call this the *anger bypass,* in the same way as someone who cries to avoid feeling other emotions is doing the *crying bypass.*

The conference itself did not interest me very much. My soul-self was growing tired of listening to other people tell me their version of what it is. It wanted me to follow my own lead.

I came home to an approved thesis. Now I had to decide if I would go on and do a PhD. Dr. Achterberg offered to be my chair. I couldn't say no. My ego wanted it. I made the decision to begin in the fall.

Suddenly my soul began to grumble. It was not happy with my decision. I began having conflicted-path dreams, yet again. In one, I was studying in a library carrel when someone attacked me with a knife. And I had a series where I was stuck in a rapidly climbing elevator. I always seemed to have this nightmare whenever I was making ungrounded decisions.

Sacred grumbles are frustrations that emanate from the soul itself, indications that the soul wants to ascend to the next stage of its evolution and that something is in the way. They can occur when we ignore our callings, walk a false path, or choose the harbors of artifice and fear over the courageous path of the soul. They can take many forms—nightmares, dark nights of the soul, physical illness, spiritual emergingcies, inexplicable negative emotions, self-sabotaging behaviors. If we ignore them, the grumbles get louder, and sometimes deadlier.

Every morning I meditated on the PhD option, listening for the language of my soul. I couldn't hear a thing. I looked to Little Missy for an answer, but she was nowhere to be found. I had to figure this one out myself.

I turned to the body of wisdom. I began a practice of charging and emptying my body prior to meditating on true-path. I began with a strong walk, run, or dance. Then I would do something emotionally expressive such as hitting the bed, crying, or expressive art until the river opened. When I felt very fluid and open, I would do a sitting or walking meditation on the question I was pondering. I did this every day until an answer emerged. I only embraced those answers that were accompanied with waves of resonance—truth chills—moving through my body. As it turned out, my body was the only authenticity-mometer I would ever need.

After many mornings like this, I heard these words: "Don't let ego decide. Let soul decide. You are not the same person anymore. You are no longer interested in the world of proofs and reason. You are on a heartier path. Let academia go."

Interestingly, I didn't experience them through the voice of Little Missy. I identified the voice as my own. I decided to defer my PhD.

Only Soul Knows

That autumn, the next career grumble arose. I began a small psychotherapy practice in my home to explore myself as a Bioenergetic therapist. Yet while working with clients, I felt like I was walking someone else's path. It wasn't the healing intention behind the work. It was the intense exercises at the heart of the model. These exercises had helped me as a client, but as a therapist I felt called to another way of working.

While putting one client over the breathing stool, my instincts were to put hands gently on her and melt her armor with kindness. This particular client had grown up in the heart of intensity. Didn't she need a gentler way of being modeled in the therapeutic process? What about tenderness as a way in, and a way out?

At the next training weekend, we went into dyads to play "therapist." I was working with an older man. As we began to work, I heard the voice of my trainer in my head: "Ground him, and then move him into his rage." I heard the call to feist, but my deeper instinct was to hold the space for him with quiet presence. I looked deeply into his eyes and asked him what he really needed right now. I asked him to trust that I wouldn't judge him. He looked me in the eyes and said, "I want to be held by you. I want to be held by a man." He lay in my arms and sobbed deeply for a long time.

That night, I walked all the way home through the city. As I walked home, I felt entirely at peace. I was happy, like a sculptor who comes home to his clay after decades of wandering. It's amazing how the body relaxes when it is on the right soul track. Equanimity Central.

I realized that in choosing Bioenergetics, I had chosen a movement that reflected my own warrior way. It was a brilliant and gutsy therapy, to be sure, but my life was now moving in the direction of surrender. I longed to develop a way of working that reflected a softer and more inquisitive perspective on reality.

After floating in and out of my own mysteries, I was growing tired of many of the psychoanalytic models. Without question, childhood experiences forge many of our defenses and patterns, but there are many other factors. What about the effects of poverty, over-stimulation, and consumerism on the development of each personality? What about genetics? What about the ways that the media forge our daily armor by deliberately putting us into fight or flight? Shouldn't we interpret behavior with these influences in mind?

Even more interesting, don't we need to inquire into how our personality patterns relate to the circumstances that our soul chose in order to grow? What the traditional psychoanalyst identifies as a problem sourced in childhood trauma, a spiritual psychotherapist might identify as the perfect grist for the soul mill. What Freud called neurosis-driven anxiety may actually be a sign that the spirit is frustrated and ready to transform. Neurotic stumbles, or growth-full grumbles? The tragic remnants of a mean-spirited mother, or welcome gifts from the divine Mother herself?

And what of the role of spirit in the therapy itself? How does a client who has known only bleakness keep the faith to do endless trauma recovery work without sensing a more positive force around her? What about introducing her to a benevolent universe? The benefits of daily spiritual practice? What about the role of our inner guidance, our daimons and angels? What about God as a buffer to hardship?

As I debated whether to leave the training, my defenses ran interference again. The Warrior berated me: "Now you are leaving another career. Why can't you finish things?" The Huckster got me worried about money. Even a dear old friend called me a quitter. Was she worried about me, or did I remind her of the explorations she was afraid to attempt?

Under what circumstances should we step off a path? When is it essential that we finish what we start? If I bought a bag of peanuts and had an allergic reaction, no one would fault me if I threw it out.

If I ended a relationship with a woman who hit me, no one would say that I had a commitment problem. But if I walk away from a seemingly secure route because my soul has other ideas, I am a flake?

The truth is that no one else can definitively know the path we are here to walk. It's tempting to listen—many of us long for the omnipotent other—but unless they are genuine psychic intuitives, they can't know. All others can know is their own truth, and if they've actually done the work to excavate it, they will have the good sense to know that they cannot genuinely know anyone else's. *Only soul knows* the path it is here to walk. Since you are the only one living in your temple, only you can know its scriptures and interpretive structure.

At the heart of the struggle are two very different ideas of success—survival-driven and soul-driven. For survivalists, success is security, pragmatism, power over others. Success is the absence of material suffering, the nourishing of the soul be damned. It is an odd and ironic thing that most of the material power in our world often resides in the hands of younger souls. Still working in the egoic and material realms, they love the sensations of power and focus most of their energy on accumulation. Older souls tend not to be as materially driven. They have already played the worldly game in previous lives and they search for more subtle shades of meaning in this one—authentication rather than accumulation. They are often ignored by the culture at large, although they really are the truest warriors.

A soulful notion of success rests on the actualization of our innate image. Success is simply the completion of a soul step, however unsightly it may be. We have finished what we started when the lesson is learned. What a fear-based culture calls a wonderful opportunity may be fruitless and misguided for the soul. Staying in a passionless relationship may satisfy our need for comfort, but it may stifle the soul. Becoming a famous lawyer is only worthwhile if the soul demands it. It is an essential failure if you are called to be a monastic this time around. If you need to explore and abandon ten careers in order to stretch your soul toward its innate image, then so be it. Flake it till you make it.

I recognized that I had walked too far down true-path to allow fearful imaginings or the opinions of others to influence my most important choices. My idea of success was now primarily soul-defined. I drove to the next training weekend and couldn't leave the car. This program had been part of my true-path, but I knew that if I walked it a moment longer, it was false-path. I went home and wrote my resignation letter. My spirit had completed this lesson. On to the next adventure.

I Got a Truth Ache

Soon thereafter I left therapy. I had been uncomfortable with it for a long time, but I had remained silent. My therapist was quite prominent in the body psychology field, and I was fearful of losing her support when I became a psychotherapist.

I would later realize the significance of these moments of truth-speak. I may have alienated a person who could help me, but I had gained the support of the divine Mother. That's what you call a good trade.

At the heart of my decision was the nagging sense that I was wasting my time in therapy. Not that I thought I had it all worked out, but I was tired of living my life through a pain portal and tired of looking for help with so many tools in my own toolbox. Either I was going to continue to turn to another to show me the way, or I was going to take responsibility for my own issues.

I plummeted back into the Rachel abyss. With no papers to write, no trainings to attend, it was back to the school of heart knocks. Somewhere inside I did sense a lesson wanting to be birthed. It came through me in the form of a *truth ache*—a nudging sense of falsity, a palpable hunger for true-path—that nagged at me now and then. I knew that the lesson was linked to the tears that I had repressed over Rachel, but it was easier to ache and grumble.

Acts of serendipity reminded me of the connection at my most detached moments. The Louisiana license plates, the feathers at my feet, that damn Sarah McLachlan song. Coming back to the feelings was essential to the lesson, whatever it was.

I made an appointment with a renowned naturopath. Inside his office, he began to examine me. Then he stopped and sat back from me. With his eyes closed he said, "They're telling me not to touch you."

I thought he was nuts. I asked him who *they* were. He said, "Your guides."

Maybe he wasn't nuts. He continued: "You had a truly great love and you have to let it go. The woman you were with was from the angelic realms. She was here to show you what lives beyond the practical world. She was here to bring you to what you are here to do. You will not marry her. She will never marry. She is here to show people all the beauty that is possible. Learn the lesson, and move on."

I left his office dumbfounded. I still carried too much pain to imagine that anything good could come from my busted-up heart, but ... what if? Was my suffering part of a cosmic plan to take me higher?

The next week I received a call off an old psychotherapy ad. The caller was a lawyer I had attended the bar admission course with. I told him that I wasn't practicing now, but he insisted on seeing me. He came to my home and told me how trapped he felt in his practice. He hadn't gone on vacation in years. He worked nearly every day and took terrible care of his body. He needed help.

From the moment he sat down, I knew that he had come as a gift. As I listened to his frustration, I saw myself writing a book about my inner journey for people caught in his range of circumstances.

Soon I began to hear that little voice inside beckoning me out of hiding. I hadn't heard from Little Missy for a while, perhaps because I hadn't needed to. When I was with Rachel, I was honoring true-path. But now that I was avoiding something, Little Missy rose to the fore. It began as a little tug at my soul string, a quiet reminder that this disappointment had fruits to bear. Then the message came stronger:

> You are distracting yourself again. Your adventure isn't over when your pleasure ends or when your expectations are not met. Your soul expands when you see each adventure through. All the way through.

Seeing it through means descending into the feelings, no matter how painful. Then the experience will reveal its true meaning. Empty yourself, and what waits in the wings will fill the space.

I went back to the couch, sweet couch. I tried to cry but I couldn't. I still wanted someone to blame—"C'mon God, why did you do this to me? Why leave me here, alone? Where are my comic-book heroes?" Although it felt hopeless, there was a lot of energy to my hopelessness. Something else was moving through the darkness.

While lying on the couch, I kept reaching for the Harbin workshop catalogue. I gravitated to a particular bodywork training—Thai-Swedish massage. I had no interest in being a body worker, but something called me to this workshop.

I couldn't imagine dealing with Harbin, where everything gets revealed. But Little Missy was a class-A nag. I could hear her inside my head: *Go to Harbin Hot Springs, Go to Harbin....* She was really pissing me off.

One night I dreamt of myself at the top of Harbin Mountain crying. A small boy came up the hill and sat beside me. He looked like me as a child, but much happier. We communed in silence for a long time. The next morning I signed up for the workshop.

10 Grist for the Soul Mill

Last night as I lay sleeping, I dreamt
Oh, marvelous error—
that there was a beehive here inside my heart
and the golden bees were making white combs
and sweet honey from all my failures.

—Joaquim Maria Machado de Assis

That summer I went into a deep, dark depression. Perhaps it is better to say that I *chose* a deep, dark depression. I felt a strong push toward my Rachel grief but still preferred avoidance. Now I took it to the next level. I stopped walking and stretching. I stopped getting massage. I ate scads of bad food. With the river all damned up, very few feelings got to the surface.

From the moment I passed Harbin's dragon gate, I knew I was in trouble. It might be good trouble, but this was not going to be easy. I pitched my tent and then went walking. Everywhere I went I was flooded with memories of Rachel. Everywhere IU.

The next morning I woke up feeling shy. This place was opening me and I wanted to hide. I walked to the restaurant. Were those people staring at me? Could they see my heartbreak? I ate two portions of sausage and eggs. I went back to my tent and curled up, reluctant to stretch myself open.

Scared Sacred

Later that day, I reluctantly showed up at the workshop. The leader was Steve Carter. He felt remarkably familiar. Yet another déjà vu. The group was very small: Steve, his assistant Lea, and three other students. No way to get lost in this crowd.

After the evening meeting, I eagerly left the building. I made two steps and heard a loud noise right beside me. It sounded like a lawn sprinkler. Something brushed against my left hand. I ran to the road and realized that I had almost walked into a rattlesnake. My heart raced as I ran up the hill to my tent.

Inside the tent, I sweated profusely. I felt claustrophobic. At first I was too agitated to sleep. Something intense was moving through me. Poison? Fear? Appreciation? When I finally slept, I had a series of macabre and twisted nightmares.

As I walked the path to the morning breathwork, I felt both scared and unusually present. It's little wonder that the words *scared* and *sacred* have only one letter switch to distinguish them. Opening the scared door had cracked me into the sacred moment.

With presence came a measure of gratitude. The rattler had terrified me more than I had realized. One more step toward it, and who knows if I would have tasted this moment? I felt powerful, like I had been called to go higher and like I actually could.

I shared my experience with the group and they congratulated me. Only at Harbin! Roberto, a true man of the Earth, said that Native Americans link the rattler to transformation. It comes to those ready to transform, to empower their journey.

Over the next few days I tried to learn Thai-Swedish massage but it was hopeless. It just didn't call me. What had I come here for? I asked Steve if I could continue even if I stopped training. He agreed. I became a massage guinea pig, worked on for hours each day. As my armor began to unpeel, my tears loomed closer. Now Rachel was close at hand.

Holding the space for this process was Steve himself. A brilliant workshop leader, he modeled the ways of a warrior of the heart. It was the first time I had met a man who so eloquently combined grace and grit. When I was near him, I felt reminded of my own innate image.

One evening Lea asked me to place my hands on her aching head. As I touched her, the inner sacred began to swell. I always know when I am in touch with a call, because I come right into my spiritual center.

Emptying the Vessel

*If you do not make it empty, how
will you fill it up again?*

—NEEB KARORI BABA

While hiking up the mountain I noticed something moving on the path. Have we met before, Mr. Rattlesnake? I moved toward him. He moved a little closer too, asserting his boundary plain and clear. I knew that I should back up, but I couldn't. I picked up a stone and threw it near him. I think I wanted the fear of death to fully wake me up to my life.

I marveled at the clarity of this powerful beast. He didn't have to worry about finding himself or becoming misidentified. He knew exactly who he was, and he lived it without hesitation. If only I could shed old layers and slip in and out of my soulskin so easily.

After some time, he slithered toward a pile of logs at the edge of the path, but not before shaking his rattle at me. Something about that rattle. Maybe it was a convenient interpretation, but was he telling me that I too could embody who I really am?

I walked to the meditation hut, closed my eyes to meditate, but I couldn't sit still. This was not a time to witness my emotions. This was a time to get lost in them. The rattler was infectious. I felt energized and powerful. I really wanted to move.

I ran through the woods at breakneck speed. Old feelings were moving through me, yearning for release. My wounds had been wrongly buried, and they longed to be liberated from their airless tomb. *Air me out!* they screamed. God, don't dam it!

I saw a hiker walking toward me from a distance. I slowed right down, containing my emotions. God forbid a stranger should see my inner world. He smiled and walked past. My fear of a stranger's judgment outweighed my love for myself. Why are we all so bloody afraid to expose our deepest truths?

I gave myself a what-for and began to run again. I ran until I gasped for air and stepped off the path. I lay down on the Earth and closed my eyes. I began to roll around on the ground, exploring my body alive. No structured yoga class for this man today. I needed to move exactly as my body demanded it.

As my body opened, deep waves of longing moved through me. I longed to touch Rachel again. I longed to feel myself move inside her. Then the anger. I raged at God. I raged at Rachel. Everything but the tears. I couldn't get to the tears.

After a soak, I walked back into the wilderness. As I walked, I inwardly repeated a new mantra: "I am going to die one day." This mantra was no death wish. It was a cry for life. By exposing the thin veil between life and death, the rattler had raised my death consciousness. I didn't want to wait until my deathbed to wake up, safe in the knowledge that my vulnerability was time-limited. I wanted to wake up now.

I went to the kirtan chant. At first I kept my breath shallow and chanted without feeling. As I souldiered on, I became lost in the breath-full sound. The reverberation of my voice shook my heartstrings loose, and a flood of emotions emerged. After kirtan I went into the warm pool and let my tears fall freely. Finally, no self-consciousness. As I cried, I felt liberated. Crying released the sweeter man who lived inside. Perhaps sensitivity isn't a sign of weakness. Perhaps it's a sign of life?

I spent the next few days opening to ever-deepening levels of soul-break. I found the just-right tree and sat against it for hours. Tears poured down from me like spring rain. I felt like I would die time and again, and then dug down for more pain. I wanted to empty it all. I wanted to breathe fresh air.

Embracing Discomfort

Only the broken wave knows the ocean.

—ROBERT AUGUSTUS MASTERS

After three days of body-washing, my heart was emptied of tension. Now I understood what depression is: frozen feeling. By stoking the heartfire, I had thawed myself out. Most significantly, this was the first time in my life that I had cried in the heart of abandonment. Rachel had left me, and I could finally grieve it.

I had been conditioned to flee my discomfort by the world around me. Ever-powerful corporate culture manipulates us away from our suffering with substitute gratifications of all kinds—comfort foods, happy movies, cozy furniture. The insidious trap of *all gain, no pain.* But true-path cannot be purchased on the highways of distraction.

In fact the entire Judeo-Christian tradition seems rooted in a subdivided version of reality. Not shadow and light, but shadow *or* light. This perspective actually embeds our darkness rather than converting it into the lessons we need. By sweeping our shadows under the rug, we hide our light under a bushel, too.

In some sense, the word *enlightenment* is misleading. It is no more about the light than the dark. In Carl Jung's words, "One does not become enlightened by imagining figures of light, but by making the darkness conscious." Resisting the shadow just makes it darker. We must turn toward it—honor the nervous breakthrough with great regard!—so that we can taste the reality that waits on the other side. It is not about becoming continuously blissful. It is about becoming more authentic, more genuinely here. It is about holding the light and the shadow all at once. Perhaps we should call the ultimate goal *enrealment*—the quest to live in all aspects of reality at once. *(Be real now.)*

Moving forward on the path demands that we develop a positive working relationship with our discomfort. In a distracted world, pain is a direct portal to the real. In addition to the lessons it teaches us, it can open the gate to Buddhaland.

Although we must honor our pain as teacher, we must also be careful for trap doors. Not all suffering is additive. Some is needless. If possible, pick your miseries with care. Time is precious.

That evening I went in for the next wave of the wake-down call: the barefoot boogie, Harbin's Thursday night dance-a-thon. It was pure Harbin—semi-naked people, conscious movement, freedom of expression.

On the dance floor I began to spin, like a determined dervish, spinning away from the familiar, spinning to God-knows-where. I got lost in the spin, doing what I had never really done—fully trusting the unknown. As I spun, I wept, and as I wept, I smiled. I went good crazy, that crazy that means vitally alive. My spin transformed into a wild dance, a cathartic quest for a place that I had yet to live. I got lost in it for hours, surrendering to the involuntary, swept away.

As I walked back to my tent, I didn't know quite who it was that was walking. My terms of reference had been left behind. In the heart of the dance, someone had fallen off of me and someone else had climbed on.

The next morning I woke up happy, perfectly happy. I finally had some gratitude in my attitude. Something sweet had come through the darkness. I went for a soak in the heart pool. Waves of bliss washed over me. I was all praise. My struggles felt like gifts that had birthed a sweeter order.

My gaze shifted from the blame-filled outer world of aggressors and pirates to the inner world of self-responsibility. With so much held inside, it had been too much to own my own piece. I had needed someone else to blame. Now I floated in the heart pool and finally asked the real questions: Why did *I* bring these circumstances into my life? Why did *I* attract a soul-mate who would crush me? What did *I* really know about the paths I had walked?

Asking these questions immediately transformed my world into a fascinating place. An annoying Harbinite came over to talk, but this time I welcomed him. I wondered, did I summon him? Had this border-crosser brought the gift of patience?

I soon found myself running through the woods again. There was something stirring inside me, and movement was the way to bring it through. I knew what it was—my soul-scriptures rising into awareness. Asking the question "How did I create my circumstances?" was the radical shift in consciousness they had been waiting for.

I ran for miles, up and down the twisty mountain road beyond the meadow. As I ran, I steamrolled the gripping self, the frightened man, the habit monger. I could feel them there, grabbing at my ankles, trying to slow me down. But they had no chance this time. The urge to emerge was too strong. I was breaking new inner ground. I felt my truth emerge a little bit more with every step.

I ran out of steam and cut off into the woods where I fell into a deep, long sleep on the forest floor.

The Guest House

This being human is a guest house.
Every morning a new arrival.
A joy, a depression, a meanness,
some momentary awareness comes
as an unexpected visitor.
Welcome and entertain them all!
Even if they're a crowd of sorrows
who violently sweep your house
empty of its furniture,
still, treat each guest honorably.
He may be clearing you out
for some new delight.
The dark thought, the shame, the malice,
meet them at the door laughing,
and invite them in.
Be grateful for whoever comes,
because each has been sent
as a guide from beyond.

—RUMI

A Sight for Soaring Eyes

Barn's burnt down, now I can see the moon.

—MASAHIDE

When I woke up I felt cohesive, as though I had been reorganized to a higher vibration. After years of painstaking work, I finally had clear eye—an unwavering bead to my center.

I walked to a high perch overlooking Harbin Valley. Tears fell down my face. Look at this magnificent valley. A sight for soaring eyes. This was God's country. Everything was God's country. How sad that we waste so much time chasing rainbows, when the rainbows live within us. Empty the inner channel and they rise into view.

Submerged in the Everything, I fell awake for … who knows how long? Time lasts forever when you are actually in the moment. Little doors opened now and then, inviting me deeper into unity consciousness. One set of eyes after another, more and more inclusive each time. Everywhere I looked, the mystery repeated itself.

I stared out over the valley and marveled at the Buddhaland that had birthed me—a tapestry of subtle and brilliant shades of meaning governed by benevolent intentionality. We are brought down this road or that, called to one lesson or the other, by a Universal Broadcasting System with a benevolent intention—the growth of the individual and universal soul … same, same.

I looked out at the real Mother of us all, the divine Mother who had never left. I had never felt her so close. Fierce but benevolent, she is always right here, breathing life into each of us, holding us safe. I sat in her lap as she breathed me. How had I failed to notice my own Mother?

If we want to really be here, we just have to open the gate to our heart. Opening the heart unlocks the heart of the universe, and we see what is always before us.

At some point I began to notice my separate self again. I was connected to the Everything, but I wasn't *identical* to everything. I had my own unique role to play in this eternal dance. The deeper I penetrated the collective soul, the closer I came to my own soul's tale.

The timeless and the timely soon intersected. I saw clear images of my life's journey. Not bits and pieces but the whole story: *archetypal wave meets localized experience.* It came through me like a film about my own life, quietly revealing, and natural—like, "Oh yah, there you are, my little story." Of course, the projector had always been inside me, only now it had a receptive audience.

As I had already gathered, our prior experiences forge our soulshape in their own image. Each lifetime presents opportunities to expand it further. Like a lake against the rocks, the shape is shifted through repeated action, carved in soulstone by the act of becoming that which we are called to be.

I set my eyes on the bigger picture: the *real* learning channel. When we are ready to stop turning a blind eye to the meaning of our experiences, we tune in to the learning channel as a way of being. Through this lens, expectations are meaningless: soul gifts come in unexpected packaging. Seeming failures can be welcome events—sometimes the ego suffers while the soul rejoices. We are knocked to the ground on the Earth plane but tripped *up* spiritually. The ladder to heaven is made of broken rungs.

One lifetime after another, the soul chooses the life that will expand its shape. It chooses its circumstances and obstacles. It chooses the nasties. It chooses the body that will best bring the lessons home. It is all essential ground to cover before we can inhabit our innate image. Without challenges, there would be no dross to convert into gold, no grist for the soul mill. *Holy* shit.

If the soul honors its path in a lifetime, it moves on to the next stage. The school of heart knocks is an ongoing university of higher learning. At some point the soul may learn all of its lessons and graduate. With no more work left to be done, it rests in the heart of Essence forever.

In my usual consciousness, I saw no connection between my circumstances and my highest paths. The difficult parents were the false-path that I had to overcome. The great love that couldn't be was just bad luck. Yet in this consciousness a deeper knowing had emerged. It turns out that I knew far more than I had been prepared to admit about the circumstances of my life. There was the superficial level of knowing, and then there was the *real* knowing.

This lifetime called for a radical transformation in my soul's consciousness. After many lifetimes as the archetypal Warrior—the call to arms—the scripture for this lifetime was to stretch into a more loving and surrendered way of being—the call to disarm.

The opportunities began with my family. I chose them because I needed them to learn my karmic lessons. I needed slaps to the head.

I needed a mother raging at me from the foot of my bed. I needed cops and debt collectors banging on the door. I needed to see the holes punched in the bedroom doors. I needed to live in a family haunted by hate.

Naturally I jumped into the fray. War was all my soul knew. And, of course, that was the idea: go to war, grow tired of war, become more open to another way of being.

Now I saw my parents for who they were. Their souls were not evil. They were just playing their part in this cosmic dance, learning whatever lessons they needed to learn and giving my soul exactly what it needed to grow forward. They were my greatest karmic teachers.

It is such an odd thing to hate people for so long, and then to recognize that they were the best thing that ever happened to you. Our lessons demand that we live through crazy things with the "monsters" in our lives, but once we have brought the lessons through, they look remarkably human, sometimes even inviting.

With grateful eyes, I saw my parents' humanness. Like so many of us, their real enemy was survivalism, the true enemy of heightened consciousness. They grew up poor and strained, then married each other and the strain intensified. Although I needed to focus on their hurtful actions to learn my own essential lessons, the truth is that they also did *many* good things, and every single act of love they performed was extraordinary given the circumstances of their lives. It is one thing for a well-nourished person to be loving, but for those who have lived such difficult lives to focus away from themselves and give love to another is a remarkable feat that resounds throughout time.

My next forum for transformation was criminal defense law. The Warrior had walked this road many times and needed to walk it one more time. There were interesting new lessons to be learned this lifetime.

This time my soul chose to work with Eddie Greenspan. I picked him because in some sense I was him. We were very similar, and watching him allowed me to witness my future. I jumped right into the madness with him. I worked hundred-hour work weeks. I ate the war game for breakfast.

There was a time in this soul's long journey when this would have been just perfect. But this life was different. Although parts of me loved the war games, other parts were already tired of it. My family life had seen to that. When the first spiritual emergingcy came my way, I was just ripe enough for the picking. As it turns out, the torrents of confusion had been a blessing, a sign that I was to move on to the next stage of my soul's journey. Who says that confusion is a bad thing?

Of course, my guardian angel, Little Missy, came down here with me. Separate yet indivisible, she sat on my shoulder and whispered sweet somethings in my ear, beckoning me to pick the right flower at the just right moment. Her job was clear: keep me on true-path, nudge me home. She had a keen eye for deviation. When I strayed from my path, she called me back. When I refused to answer, she brought the message through in other ways.

My next forum for transformation was Rachel. As I looked out over the valley, I saw our hearts asking for love months before we met. I saw the universal ear listening with an open heart. I saw our guiding angels jumping into action to bring it our way. Now I understood why I knew she would be in Boulder. She was so intrinsic to my innate image that I could see her coming from a thousand miles away.

The lesson itself came through the heart. Little Missy led this (war) horse to water and then brought him the temptress that he could not help but drink. She knew that the antidote for the Warrior was love — bring him his soul-mate and he will never be the same. She knew that I would have never taken the love bait earlier, in the tear-down stages of self-creation, before I had established the girders necessary to stand in the fire.

In Rachel's presence, my Warrior soul abandoned its armor and fell to its knees. Every time I opened, I dove deeper into the broader universe, love's liquid lava flowing from the heart to the genitals to the great beyond. The more I lingered there, the more I entrenched a surrendered way of being.

Little had I known that the opportunity was not the love itself but what came later. To become the surrendered man that I had identified as my innate image, I had to do more than lose at love. I had to embody the depths of my heartbreak. If not, the Warrior would return with a vengeance and it might take another dozen lifetimes before he could surrender again.

Here at Harbin my soul made its choice. It chose living in the light over living in the might. By embracing my discomfort, I had converted my pain into the lessons held within it. By re-opening my heart when it was most difficult, I realized surrender as a way of being. As it turned out, there had been no love lost between Rachel and me. There was only love's labor found—everywhere a white flag with a heart at its center. By leaving me, she had made my heart my home.

Now I saw why it could never have happened any other way. It doesn't matter how much two people love one another if they are developmentally incompatible, or if there is not a shared willingness to become conscious. This is why they call it a relationship instead of a loveship. Love alone is not enough. If you want it to last, you have to relate to each other in ways that keep the ship afloat. Although we had loved each other deeply, the psychological girders were simply not there to support a lasting relationship. We were supposed to touch wings, and then fly away.

Cell Your Soul

Bringing our soul lessons through takes more than awareness. It is an active process that demands a courageous willingness to live our experiences right through to completion. This means staying with our feelings until they are truly done with us, no matter how uncomfortable it is. Although we may not see it at first, there is a method to our sadness.

Oftentimes we distract ourselves out of the learning, particularly when the feelings are painful. We all know people like this. We have all been people like this. We choose not to get the hint. We ignore our grumbles and truth aches at all costs. If we don't break this habit, we just come back the next time with the same lessons waiting in the wings.

The body is far more than just a vessel for the soul. It is the field where the soul's lessons are harvested. It is the breeding ground for the soul's emergence. In order to grow forward, we must bring our suffering through our emotional body until our spiritual lesson is birthed. We must *cell our soul.*

The recipe is simple. Be authentic and true to your felt experience. Feel the heartbreak. Feel the anger. Feel all of your feelings. If you had a cruel father, move your anger and feel into the heartbreak below. If you lose a loved one, go through all the stages of grieving. Don't stop halfway. Never stop halfway. Let the feelings tell you if the fire was destructive or benevolent. Some fires are creating the way for new life.

Be careful not to go into your head. There is a meaningful difference between a cerebral interpretation of an experience ("I *know* why this came into my life") and an embodied awareness of it ("I *feel* why this came into my life"). Unless your knowing arises from your felt experience, it is meaningless. Stay with the emotional process until your soul food is digested. It will be difficult at times, but the feelings will only hurt until they convert. *Repressed emotions are unactualized spiritual lessons.* Once they make it all the way through the conversion tunnel, the spiritual lesson will be revealed. Divine perspiration.

The Fire of Essential Light

As I sat inside myself, I knew that I had become the surrendered man I had seen by the fire of essential light. For this moment at least, I saw the world through his eyes. Through them, I opened to the next stages of my journey. My path did not end here. The next scriptures were waiting at the gate to unfold.

My callings began to flash before me. What a surprise—I had seen them all before! What a surprise—all that stumbling in the dark had been grounded in a deeper knowing. By becoming a surrendered man, I could now do the work I was called to do. This loving work was the gift back to the universe that every soul longs to make.

At the heart of my callings was the presumption of Essence. I was here to invite others to surrender to Essence and to ask the real questions of their lives: Who am I, really? What are my soul-scriptures? Why am I here?

The most pressing call was to write my first book—this book, the story of one person's struggle to identify and honor his entelechy amid the minefields of misidentification. It was the story that I had lived, or that had lived me, being used as karmic fodder for the mill of human expansion. I saw myself sitting on the floor in the back room of my house, writing it.

I saw myself writing other books as well, including an uncommon-bond love story. In that book, the couple would get lost in the triggers as Rachel and I had, but they would take a different path. Instead of turning away from the fire, they would do the work to heal the issues that kept them apart. They would fight tooth and nail for their gateway to God.

I also saw myself working as a body-centered psychotherapist, perhaps one day constructing an approach that integrated more subtle and surrendered ways of working into the therapy.

Although the images were clear, it was also clear that it didn't have to happen in exactly these ways for me to live a complete life. There were ways that better honored my gifts, to be sure, but the key was the intention behind it. The key was staying true to the surrendered heart, wherever that path might lead.

All the hurts and failures, all the wanderings, losings, dyings, and forgettings were but part of the gaining of the rich material of your life. By being wounded you became vulnerable and available; by being lost, you were able to be found; by dying you learned the power of new birth; by forgetting, you gained the joy of remembering. Now I call all parts of you back, a mighty crew, seaworthy and well stocked, to set sail for new continents of spirit, shores of incredible lands where the fractal waves of many people and many times arrive at last, and you know that you have gained your birthright. Welcome back, God and Goddess, no longer in hiding.

—JEAN HOUSTON

---

11 Bridge Crossings

To change, a person must face the
dragon of his appetites with another
dragon, the life-energy of the soul.

—RUMI

With my soul-scriptures under my arm, I rode the bus from Harbin to San Francisco in a meditative state. Ideas for this book moved through me all the way to the Mission Street Station. I arrived and took a hellish cab ride to Haight-Ashbury. I had forgotten about this rough-and-tumble world, the "real" world of tin machines and armored hearts.

I walked all afternoon, overwhelmed by urban life. Be *here* now? Yuck! After two weeks of near-perfect diet, I went straight for the pizza slice. Bring on the wheat and cheese! I wondered if it was just me or if urban life was always out of step with a soulful life. Haven't I already answered this question?

I took a taxi to the airport. The driver gave me attitude. I went inside the airport wasteland to check my bags. The attendant gave me attitude. As I walked to the ticket window, a wild man banged up against me. How to breathe all this in?

I sat down to wait. The frenetic energy of the airport crept in on me. Suddenly I wanted a strong coffee—jet fuel for the night flight home, or some illusion like that. A conservative older man sat down beside me and started to talk. I asked him how to stay real in the heart of this madness. He looked at me like I was mad and said, "Grin and bear it, boy." Survivalist mantra. I got up and moved.

I boarded the plane feeling anxious. The plane took off into the dark night sky. I looked out the dark window all the way home, fretting. I thought about my daily life in Toronto. I began to question my callings. Through the eyes of survivalism, callings can seem like flights of fancy, impractical notions with dangerous consequences. Could I stay attuned to my higher purpose in the heart of modern life? Could I make the presumption of Essence in everyday life?

The next day I sat down in a city park and stumbled upon a story just longing to be told. I wrote until long after I could see the paper I wrote on. I had two wonderful weeks, walking and writing on air. Words that had been waiting at the gate for years raced onto the page, stumbling into one another mid-sentence. Often I would write for a few days before feeling hungry. This is in the nourishing nature of our callings once they are set free and expressed. Sometimes they feed the body all on their own.

Karmageddon

On September 8, 2001, I had a dream. An Arabic pilot hijacked an American Airlines jet and crash-landed it on my street, just missing my house. Persuaded by the common misconception that dreams are exclusively about the dreamer, I interpreted it as a sign that I was finally piloting my own ship and out of harm's way. It didn't occur to me that my dream could be an expression of someone else's intentions.

On September 10, I fell happily asleep in the arms of Little Missy. Peace with path. I woke the next morning to a message from my grandmother to turn on the television. I should have refused. The first test.

Initially, the sight of people jumping from the smoldering towers cracked me deeper into the moment. I was again *scared sacred*, frightened into the heart of unity consciousness. I was the jumpers, the perished, the New Yorkers running for their lives. I was even the pilots. It was our mutual drama.

I couldn't leave the television. I hated the suffering but longed for something in the heart of it. Every image of horror was a depth charge that excavated my love for humanity a bit more. My heart opened wide, wider still.

After a few days, the space that had opened inside me closed in on itself. I found myself swimming in a narrow little fear stream, blind to the bigger ocean. My body tightened and armored, readying for war. I became hyper-vigilant, looking for the enemy everywhere. Better to keep one eye on the television screen and another on the front door, just in case.

In the heart of it, I heard my inner knowing nudging me to write. But there was such a tension between my creativity and this desperate state of being. It was like trying to write a love letter with a gun at my head.

One afternoon I decided that this book was frivolous. Most of humanity was dealing with basic needs and hungers. Was it not indulgent, even insensitive, to dwell on my own inner journey? *Who* was I kidding?

This was my first real glimpse into the challenge of actualizing a soulful calling in a harsh landscape. I was trying to step across a shaky bridge that traversed two very different landscapes: gross and subtle ways of being. If I was completely lodged on either side, I would not be as confused by these events. But I was still shedding my survivalist orientation, and I had not yet consolidated a more subtle soulshape. It was going to be a challenging crossing.

After some time, I remembered the practice that had served me well. I reluctantly turned off the television and went back to the cabin. Here I could see beyond the veils of my usual jurisdiction. As I walked through the woods, my body slowly surrendered, clenched hands ungripped, heart opened. The soldier consciousness faded from view.

One of the best ways to deal with our tendency to armor is to bring our patterns of armoring into consciousness. Although there are times when armoring is essential to our well-being, we often put it on when we don't need it, or we keep it on for too long. Consider the possibility of dialoguing with your soul-self both when you choose to armor: ("I have to shut down right now; I promise I will be back as soon as I can") and when you come back to openness ("I am back; I missed you").

There is a lot to be said for making all of our adaptations conscious. *Conscious adaptation* is the idea that we choose our adaptations with awareness, for a limited time and clearly defined purpose. We approach it like an actor doing a role. We know who we are, we know who we must become in order to get the job done, and we remember to take our mask off as soon as the performance is over. By making our adaptations conscious, we move away from the grips of survivalism as a way of life, and closer to an Essence-centered reality.

I soon reconnected with the beauty of this Mother Earth. Things began to sparkle and shine, and I stumbled back upon my passionate purpose in the heart of it. At the babbbbling brook, the call whispered into my inner ear: "There is work to be done on every frontier. Honor your path faithfully. Get back to the book." The *souldier* was back in business.

Jumping the Light

I came home swept away by the call to write, surrendering to a month-long wave of words. It was a magnificent experience in letting go, letting in, letting out. I broke off from the small self-perception that had plagued me for most of my life. I glimpsed my true brilliance and worth. I saw a beautiful being dipping his pen in a wellspring of eternal light.

At the end of that month, I began to retreat. It wasn't the challenge that turned me away. It was the ease. When it was difficult I stayed and fought it out. Yet when there was nothing to strive for, when I felt magnificent and alight, I shut myself down with *depth-avoidant behaviors:* reading the racing form, renting bad videos, sleeping with the wrong women. Abraham Maslow had an interesting name for it— *Jonah Complex*—or the fear of our own greatness. We touch into our magnificence and then run for the hills.

I challenged myself to connect to the feelings that sourced my resistance. The primary thing that surfaced was a profound fear of exposure. Shame still slept very close to the throne of my actualizing self, listening in for that moment when I imagined myself relevant. If I kept myself small, it stayed asleep. But if I imagined myself useful, the shame-a-thon began. I found myself sitting at the computer, simultaneously writing and mocking my writing: "You are so narcissistic. Who are you to believe that you can write? Do you think anyone cares about your story?"

Money and security issues became the next challenge to the creative process. For a long time, I lived comfortably on three long sales days per week, leaving plenty of time to write. But my small business was running out of steam. In order for it to survive, I would have to sell windows full-time.

I postponed the inevitable for as long as I could but woke up one morning gripped with fear. The Huckster had returned to remind me of where I came from and where I might go if I didn't get back in the game. I got up to write, but the voice was buried below a money-mind swirl of calculation and anxiety.

I considered leaving the marketplace altogether. Countless others had risked it all to follow their bliss. Some of their stories had inspired my own journey. But after all those years of basic-needs alarm, I was still attached to the illusion of security. To pacify the Huckster, I needed a house, a good income, and a solid retirement plan.

I was still lodged in the belief that I was either in my real self and not making money, or in my false-self making a living. Never the twain could meet. I decided to alternate sales and writing phases over four-month periods.

After a few weeks of full-time sales, I became indistinguishable from the fast-talking Huckster. Survivalism lends itself to a disguised life—anything to pay the bills! Lost to the money game, I began buying silly things. It made perfect sense. When I was writing, honoring my call gratified me. But sales was not my true calling. It fed my body but not my soul. I gravitated toward substitute gratifications in the absence of real ones.

After three months I had made enough money to cover my economic needs for the next four months. Actually, I had technically made enough money after two months, but I needed another month to recoup substitute gratification expenditures. That's the thing about wasted money—it forces you to stay in your false-self that much longer just to earn it back.

When the time came to return to writing, I couldn't find the voice. I went right back out there and continued selling. I was imprisoned by my own adaptations. One night I had a key nightmare. I was on an elevator, dressed in a frou-frou suit, on the way up to a fancy night-club. The elevator began to fall at breakneck speed. On the way down,

I had only one mortifying thought: I am going to die and I am not even here! The elevator hit the ground and spiraled downward into the deep dark earth.

The meaning was immediately obvious. When I had started to sell, there was little dissonance because earning money was an essential aspect of my journey. I couldn't ascend without honoring my basic needs, and mine included lots of financial stability. But in continuing to sell after meeting my needs, I had gone well beyond grounded pragmatism. Now I was so grounded on the Earth plane that I was essentially buried in it. From way down here I couldn't see the sky or access spiritual experience. Everything was pragmatism: the *material bypass.*

I went out for one more day of business and then ended the selling phase. After a few days back at the computer, the writing voice kicked in. I wrote strong and free for a month, then went to the Omega Center for a psychotherapy training led by Ron Kurtz.

As I listened to Ron introduce *Hakomi,* my soul grumbled. Where before I tended to elevate my teachers, I now felt frustrated with being a student. It felt too safe and disempowering, like I was hiding here from the responsibilities and risk attached to my own power. Why was I listening to his voice when mine was eager to be expressed? I stayed until the first break and drove straight back to Toronto to write.

That summer, memories of early suffering arose to haunt me. Something about sitting in the light of the call triggered things shadowy back to the surface. God, does this well ever run dry? Then Little Missy uttered what would become my mantra amid the minefields of distraction: "Push on through with your call even when the resistance tempts you away. Surrender to the call and it will become indistinguishable from you."

I sat down at the computer to "push on through." Then after three months I ran out of money. I turned off the computer and resumed my selling phase. But this time my soul grumbled like wildfire. After months pushing on through, I couldn't live without my writing. Every few days I had to sit down at the computer just to feel connected.

I decided to write in the morning *and* sell in the afternoon. It was the first time that my hunger to survive could not completely dominate my call. This was both a liberating and frightening moment. It was liberating because my spiritual life refused to say die. It was frightening because my spiritual life refused to say die.

Friends Fall Away

Inner growth is like a truth serum that re-frames and clarifies our lens to the outside world. Our social life is one of the things that must change to accommodate our expansion and reflect our new ways of being. It is in the nature of soulshaping to want to trade up as our consciousness expands.

As I honored my call, my relationships with others dramatically changed. In one sense I felt more intimately connected to all of humanity. The call pulled me out of an isolated self-sense and reminded me that we are all part of the same inextricable web of life. Through these eyes, there were no strangers.

At the same time, I didn't seem to need as much social contact as before. I didn't long for contact to fill me up or to distract me from reality. My romance with my own soul engaged me more than most social experiences, and waves of unity consciousness ensured that I never felt completely alone.

Friends fell away as I individuated on my soul's journey. As I shed one self-sense, I no longer identified with the people attached to it. Old ways of interacting seemed artificial, scripted, silly. Whereas before it was fine to hang out and waste time, now there was no time to lose. Now I had to protect my higher purpose from connections that undermined it.

At first I didn't want to face the impossibility of certain connections. I preferred to make myself small in order to sustain them. I think of it as sinking to the lowest common denominator. If two people cannot meet on relatively equal footing, there are two options: the relationship can end, or it can be organized around the developmental stage of the least conscious member.

My clinging had many roots, with guilt as the kingpin. The nature of it was akin to "survivor guilt," except that no one had died. I refer to it instead as *survivalist guilt*, the guilt we might experience when we shift from survivalism as our primary orientation toward a subtle and essential way of being. At the heart of the guilt is the survivalist mantra: *We all stick together.* Huddling together for dear life, we honor those who got us here, regardless of their limitations. Like many who attended the school of heart knocks, I was loyal to my brethren.

Intensifying my loyalty was a misguided humanism. I had yet to learn that it is possible to hold the belief in someone else's highest possibilities while simultaneously accepting that they are not at a stage where a friendship is appropriate. Because growth-oriented individuals tend to be empathic, they run a particular risk of remaining close to people who can drag them down.

After some time, my impatience with incongruent friends overwhelmed me. The transition was strange. While eating breakfast with a particularly narcissistic friend, I felt the desire to throw it at him. I was tired of losing myself at the breakfast table. Of course, it wasn't really him that I was angry at. It was the part of myself that he reminded me of. Sometimes we end relationships because we are trying to outgrow those parts of ourselves that the other reflects. We need to get away from these identifications so that others can concretize.

One day I encountered one of my employees. Robert was a light-challenged kind of guy, a dark and difficult person to connect with. It was all small talk—the kind of talk that keeps everyone small. He never asked about me, and he always used anything I said as an immediate jumping-off point for his own stories.

I asked how he was doing, and he went on about his friend: "My buddy has three Mercedes, he's really made it." I said, "That's three too many. What does he need them for?" No answer. We weren't resonating. I asked him how he felt about his friend's success. No answer. Not supposed to ask about feelings. I searched my inner database to see if there was a way to bridge to him without falsifying myself. I did the divine Mother thing and tried to see him in all his wholeness but it was difficult.

He went into a story about his beer-drinking exploits. After fifteen more minutes, I heard an angry voice from within pounding in my inner ear: "Stop the lie. Not one more false word." Then, in the heart of one of my own bullshit sentences, I abruptly stopped speaking: "Yeah, nothing like a beer...." I just walked away. I couldn't bear to hear myself so small. It was disrespectful to Robert, but it was a groundbreaking moment in my relational life. It's never rude to interrupt your false-self.

I became especially boundaried around those who undermine positive intentionality in others: *lite-dimmers*. While doing so, I always tried to stay in compassion. The key was to recognize that they were simply stuck at a certain point in the journey—the narcissist was just someone who had yet to be heard, the space invader was still learning about boundaries, the perpetual distracter was still afraid of his depths. It wasn't that difficult to be empathic. I had been all of these styles of relating at different times.

I got comfortable with falling away from people in my life. The dividing line seemed to be those who were genuinely interested in the inner journey and those who fled it like a tornado. I often imagined myself climbing a mountain. In the lower valleys there was plenty of oxygen to sustain the climb. It was fine to carry the baggage of the ones who couldn't find their own footing yet. Yet as I ascended, the oxygen level decreased. I could only carry those things that met my basic needs or energized me. Anything else would hold me back. I would close my eyes and imagine the person in question: Did they energize me as I attempt to climb the higher peak, or did they cause my knees to buckle? If the latter, I had to limit or sever the connection.

The most difficult fall-away has been my father. It has little to do with past traumas or angers. It has everything to do with my own changes. Sometimes I see him walking and it feels horrible to drive by without stopping. I know what is in store for me if I do stop, and I know that it won't benefit anyone, but it still feels terribly sad. It all works out fine if each generation progresses one tiny step ahead of the generation before. But it is more challenging when the apple falls a little farther from the tree.

There can be tremendous loneliness in the crossover to a soul-centered life. Walking through uncharted territory often means walking alone. This is particularly true in the transition stages before we find a conscious soulpod. It can be like primary school all over again—who will be my first *real* friends?

Selective Attachment

The light of the call grew stronger. Sweet little soul forms began to work their way through the money man. In the middle of signing business deals, I would hurriedly write down book ideas on the bottom of contracts for fear I would forget. Sometimes I was late for appointments because I had to stop and fill my answering machine with book ideas. The creative and practical modalities were beginning to merge.

Then my busy lifestyle closed in on me. I had been writing and selling almost every day, and I was also working as a therapist one day per week.

I felt the temptation to journey back to nature to find my center, but this time I resisted. Now that I had a clearer sense of why I was here, the next step was learning how to hold to it anywhere.

I identified two primary needs for a soulful life in the heart of the city: *spaciousness* and *congruence.* The more congruent my choices were with true-path, the more spacious my inner world. The more space inside, the easier it was to make congruent choices.

To create a more congruent and spacious reality, I was guided by the principle of *selective attachment.* In the context of soulshaping, selective attachment is the process of sifting everything through an essential filter, connecting only to those experiences and relationships that support true-path. If something supports our ascension, we bring it on. If it doesn't, we stay away. We endeavor to make soul-serving choices at every turn.

In the Buddhist tradition, there is much emphasis placed on non-attachment. In the words of the Dalai Lama, "Attachment is the origin, the root of suffering; hence it is the cause of suffering." To come to God, you separate yourself from the world around you. Conversely, the Sufi tradition emphasizes the art of involvement. Rather than separating ourselves from the world, we jump right into the madness and find God in the heart of it. The Dervish spins his way to God.

Selective attachment is the middle way. We embrace the idea that certain desires and attachments are healthy and soul-affirming under the right circumstances: How will we learn our lessons if we do not get involved? What is wrong with pleasure as a path? How to not attach to someone we love? And we embrace the idea that non-attachment is the right path at other times: Why stay connected in the heart of unbearable suffering and needless discomfort? Is separation not essential to individuation?

The first need—spaciousness—was my most pressing. After an early life filled with intrusive people, I needed space! Space served as the buffer between my subtle center and the outer world.

Space came in many forms: physical, energetic, and emotional.

At this time, my greatest obstacle to spaciousness was the pace and complexity of my daily life. If I wasn't doing one thing, I was doing another thing faster. I actually took pride in how many things I could do in an afternoon. Breathing was not one of them.

The busier I was, the more burnt-out I felt. The more burnt-out I felt, the more I spent on distractions and vacations. The more I spent, the more burnt-out I became earning the money to pay for them. Modern madness.

I began to experiment with a more simplified way of being, modeling aspects of my daily life on the simpler world that my grandparents had known. I established a pattern of simplifications that served me well. For example, I de-cluttered my physical environment. Because I grew up poor, a house filled with things was a buffer against those old feelings of never enough. Now I went through my house with a fine eye, inquiring into whether those attachments enhanced or cluttered my life. In a cluttered room, I felt locked into a cluttered mindset. In a spacious room, space opened up inside me.

I attempted to bring the same bare-bones intention to my spending habits. The trick was to identify the fine line between material comfort and material trappings. To contain my daily spending, I did little walk-abouts before making a purchase. Big savings, those walk-abouts. I would put the items down and walk until I got clear. One afternoon I stood in a store lineup with my arms filled with clothes. I just had to have a new wardrobe before writing about my naked soul, right? Luckily, it was a long line. I got frustrated and went for a walk. That walk saved me six hundred dollars I didn't need to spend.

Purchases are simply energetic exchanges. The only thing that distinguishes one from another is the intention behind it. We need to distinguish those purchases that serve our spiritual life from those that undermine it. *Unconscious consumerism* is making purchases in order to avoid the real. We are doing the material *buy-pass* in an effort to sidestep the deeper work. *Conscious consumerism* is about making exchanges that take us higher. This can include anything that meets our genuine needs (my grandmother truly *did* need her first couch in order to feel a part of the world) or that gives us soulful satisfaction. Anything that takes us closer to our innate image. Like everything, our consumerism is only as healthy as the intention behind it.

I also worked hard to avoid the world of commitments—*the oblig-nation*. I made fewer personal plans generally, and those that I did make were often spontaneous. This allowed me to be truer to myself in each moment. Why go if you aren't going to *really* be there? Keep it simple. Keep it real.

The second need was that of congruence. To remain soul-connected in modern life, it was essential that I selectively attach to people, places, and activities congruent with my authentic self. Incongruent structures dragged me down. Congruent structures invited me higher.

I began with incongruencies. I worked with the body scan to identify them. If I knew one thing, it was that my soul grumbled right through my body if I dishonored it.

The scan began with my breath: Is my breath contracted or expanded in the heart of an experience? I scanned my energy: Am I energetically engaged? I scanned my anatomy: Is my body relaxed or tightened? I scanned my body language: Are my feet on the ground or am I pulling up and out of the experience? I scanned my emotional body: Am I joyous? Angry? Ready to scream? Is my heart open?

Where possible, I consciously avoided incongruent experiences. Of course, it wasn't possible to sever completely. We have to drive in tiresome traffic, line up at the bank, attend family functions. In these situations, I did my best to stay connected to my essential self. In traffic, I listened to New Age music to keep me open. At uncomfortable family gatherings, I lay down in another room and connected to my breath. Sometimes I actually talked to my soul-self and asked it how it was doing. Call me crazy, it actually helped. These little *soul breaks* became a buffer against the madness of the world.

Perhaps the most effective buffer was participating in my writing itself. I continued to deepen my practice of staying with my writing no matter how distracted I felt. When I did this, those things that were incongruent with the real me didn't tempt me as readily.

12 Ascending with Both Feet on the Ground

Every moment I shape my destiny with a
chisel—I am the carpenter of my own soul.

—RUMI

It became apparent that removing incongruencies wasn't enough. I also needed to selectively attach to activities congruent with my true nature. I began with little adjustments—peaceful restaurants, city picnics, quieter streets. These helped, but there was something missing.

What was missing was energy. Without meeting the energetic demands of urban life, I fell back into my false-self time and again. I walked out of massages feeling emotionally open and shut back down soon after getting into the car. I needed an energetic boundary to protect me and to keep me moving forward.

If You Can't Stand the Heat, Get Out of the Kirtan!

I gravitated toward practices that would keep me both open and energized. I began with ashtanga, a power yoga that moves through asanas or poses fairly quickly. When I practiced traditional hatha yoga, I thought my way through class. When I practiced ashtanga, I had to breathe deeply to keep pace, and my energy dropped down and enlivened my body. I loved it.

When too much ashtanga began to give me mat rage, I added restorative yoga to my practice. In restorative, one spends much of the time lying on the floor, holding poses for long periods. I began to weave restorative poses into my ashtanga classes and to do at least one restorative class every week. It was the perfect balance—ashtanga gave me the charge to meet daily demands, and restorative helped me to recover from those demands.

Interestingly, yoga also became a tool for emotional healing. As my practice deepened, feelings trapped within various holdings rose to the surface, demanding expression and release. This was particularly true when I pushed myself to do those asanas I disliked the most. I began to leave a little private time after class for honoring my emotions.

There was a beautiful relationship between yoga and the call to write. Often I would do a class when I felt tight inside. The tighter I felt, the farther I drifted away from the creative source spring. Yet as the class progressed, space would open inside and my call would surge right back into consciousness.

After my body began to strengthen, my ego briefly took over my yoga practice. I became competitive with the other students in the class. I wrote cool spiritual sayings on my yoga mat. I signed up for yoga workshops just so I could say that I had signed up for yoga workshops. I was soulshopping, attempting to bypass the real work by purchasing spirituality in the marketplace.

Of course, the only thing that spiritualizes a moment is the intention to get real. If we do a beautiful thing with a superficial intention, we do a superficial thing. The genuineness of our experience is determined by the genuineness of our intention.

I straightened myself out. I stopped writing on my mat and I began calling myself on my egoic intentions in the heart of class. Now whenever I catch myself comparing my asanas to others (I usually lose), I go down into child's pose until I reconnect with a purer intention.

My inner flashlight soon uncovered the next source of energy— live food. I noticed that after many meals, I couldn't find the energy to write. It took every bit of energy to process one sandwich. Something was shutting me down.

I investigated and recognized that it was cooked food that was depleting my energy by draining me of all my digestive enzymes. To put it simply, dead foods deaden us. Instead of gaining more energy to meet life, all of our energy goes to digesting the indigestible. I had accepted this as normal, having turned to over-the-counter digestive aids to help me along. Of course, if store-bought digestive aids were the answer, we would have an organ manufacturing them.

Instead of interpreting the body's reactions as information on how to live and structure our society, we work it like a mule until it becomes so ill that we are forced to listen in. In fact the body has all the answers we need. We just need to learn how to ask it the right questions. If we don't take care of the temple, there will be no place to pray.

I began to look for natural energy sources. I turned to live food. Live meals enlivened me and stoked my creative energy higher. They also gave me tremendous clarity and focus. After lunch I sat at the computer for hours without missing a beat.

Properly used, live foods expand our connection to the moment and nourish our spiritual path. They are like the sun shining from the inside out. The more pure and vital our body, the more alive we are to spirit. The more spirited we are, the more our body opens and energizes.

Despite this burgeoning energy, there were still places that I couldn't go inside. Because of my rigid tendencies, I needed an energizing practice to shake me loose.

I naturally gravitated toward *kirtan chant*. The heat of the chant had melted my armor at Harbin years before, and I felt ready to surrender to its teachings. Commonly practiced in India, kirtan is the repetitive chanting or singing of God's names. Intrinsic to the bhakti path (the path of devotion), it invites us to shed our ego armor and nestle into a bigger consciousness.

Because we are culturally conditioned to be seen and not heard, we forget that sounding is essential to our well-being. When we repress our self-expression, we dam the inner river at its source. When we chant strongly, we can bring ourselves back to life. The sound vibrations chisel away at the walls of our emotional holdings, shaking our heartstrings loose.

Chanting became an integral part of my daily life and a wonderful tool to stoke my authentic self higher. I began to chant everywhere, all the time. I woke up to Deva Premal on my disc alarm. I chanted in the car, on the plane. I spent five wondrous days at a Krishna Das retreat at Paradise Island. I wrote listening to Wah, Wade Morrisette, Jennifer Berezan, and the so beautiful Swaha.

With so much energy channeled toward my calling, my personality began to change. Most significant was the new personality that emerged in my business dealings. The light of the call elevated my attitude and infused my personality with light. Instead of strong-arming people into deals, I sold with a gentler touch, seeing people as God, selling with God. To my utter surprise, I made the same money with kindness that I had made with warrior intensity.

Finding My Soulpod

... admirable friends, admirable
companions, admirable comrades. This is
the first prerequisite for the development
of the wings to self-awakening.

—THE BUDDHA

I began to long for social contact. Letting your soul be your pilot often means that you fly solo until you are ready for deeper connection. The last group of incongruent friends had fallen away, and I was now ready to connect from a more conscious place. I also knew that I couldn't get to the next stage of my ascension alone.

When I was less individuated, it was easier to make friends. The more amorphous we are, the easier it is to find someone to hang out with. It may not be as deeply gratifying, but there is always someone to have a drink with. But now I didn't want to just have a drink. I wanted to be met in the deep within.

I characterized this longing as the quest for my soulpod. Our soulpod is that person or group of people whom our soul finds the most resonance with at any given moment. It can include anyone that appears on our path to inform and catalyze our expansion—our biological family, significant figures, strangers with a lesson. In the words of soul archaeologist Tarini Bresgi, members of our soulpod are like pop-ups that appear on our path to smooth the rough edges of our soul. How long they stay depends on the scripture. It could be a moment, it could be a lifetime.

I wanted to connect with a soulpod of people walking the same soul beat—less ego, more Essence. Heartfelt friends sitting around the hearth of essential light with our souls on our sleeves. Where to find them?

Over the next few years, I found them everywhere. I made new friends at yoga studios and holistic centers. I pushed myself to make contact with people who felt resonant, no matter the circumstances. It was all in the eyes. I identified like-spirited others by looking into their eyes.

One member of my biological family crossed the bridge with me. My grandmother had been an essential figure in my birth pod, grounding and nourishing me amid the battlegrounds of early life. This would have been enough. Yet through new eyes I recognized that the vulnerable little lady at the head of my family was also a member of my consciousness pod. She also fought for the open heart amid the distractions of daily life.

In this process, we must have faith that we will survive that often-lonely space between old friends falling away and new ones showing their face. This faith is our buffer against the temptation to go back to the familiar. If we can hang tight and make conscious efforts to connect, the next pod will be walked in our direction when the moment is right. We call to them, they call to us, and our angels broker the deal.

No Return

With yoga, chant, and live food to energize me, I walked much farther along true-path. I wrote strong and free for many months, without fanfare.

Then came a radical shift in my economic situation. After a downturn in the marketplace, my bad check pile had more than doubled. I was in considerable debt for the first time in fifteen years of business.

I put *Soulshaping* away and went back to selling windows full-time to cover the debt. For a few weeks, there was nothing but moneymaking in my mind's eye. One night I ended a long hard day of business with an excellent sales contract. I left the customer's house to go home, but I couldn't start the car. I lay down in the car right in front of their house and heard these words: *Have faith that all you need is already here.*

The next morning I got up to go to work but I couldn't go. I missed this book too much. By expressing it, I came into being. My calling had reached a stage where it could not be extinguished altogether: the shape of no return. It was now deep in my cells that the only *real* enemy was separation from my call. Even if the Huckster was right and I would die of starvation if I didn't sell glass day and night, what choice did I have? If I stopped honoring the call, I died too. Better to die true.

As we honor our calling, we grant it more space inside of us. Light begets light—at a certain point, there is no way to escape the inner beacon. Our calling begins to soak every aspect of our lives, whatever the cost or inconvenience. We cannot live without our call because our call has become us. Path decisions then come straight from the heart of true-path, and we move only when our soul motor tells us to.

The soul has a no-return policy. Once we cross a certain point in our expansion, we can't go back.

I returned to a balanced working life, writing in the mornings and selling in the daytime. I felt the pinch of the accumulated debt but felt peaceful despite it—the peace that comes from knowing that you will not sacrifice true-path to the devils of artifice and materialism. It is a strange faith, not simply that the universe will provide for you, but that *you* will provide for you. The only *real* homeland security is the knowledge that whatever the world brings your way, your soul is safe in your own two hands.

Soon I was blessed with another challenge to the honoring of this call. I asked a friend to recommend a literary agent for this book. He recommended a leading agent. I spoke to her, and she asked for an outline. While preparing it, I had mixed feelings. Part of me was really charged up about it. My ego began to trip out. Foot in the door, great opportunity, all that. Below this, it felt like a big waste of time. It was still the first draft, and I had no idea what form it would be in when I got to the end. Even worse, I felt like I was adjusting the book to my idea of what someone else wanted to read.

Not surprisingly, it was not accepted. Perfect lesson in trusting your inner knowing. I had others look at it, and they said this book is too painfully subjective to appeal to people. No one wants to read about someone's miserable journey of self-creation. The outer journey of plane-crash survival, maybe. But not the inner one.

This situation was superficially different from the debt challenge, but in both cases I was asked to decide how imperative it was to be true to my soul voice. To what extent would I allow my call to be influenced and shaped by the marketplace?

I sat with it for a while and the answer came clear. It was an old answer. If societal success were my deal this time around, I'd be kicking ass in a courtroom for three thousand dollars a day instead of sitting at this computer. Honoring my scripture meant honoring it to the letter. It demanded a subjective account. It was going to get a subjective account, the marketplace be damned.

Some say, "Do what you love and the money *will* follow." This is a misleading aphorism that only applies to some. "Do what you love and the money *may* follow" is more realistic. Some of us follow a path that does not generate an adequate income on its own, but we are called to follow it nonetheless. We have to do what we came here to do even if it means that we make our money doing something else.

Sacred Balance

Crossing over into no return seemed to be the catalyst for remarkable changes within me. One weekend I went to see Bhagavan Das chant at a downtown yoga studio with a giant neon mall right behind it. As the sun went down, the image of Bhagavan Das chanting began to darken and fade and the neon signs behind him became more prominent.

Where before I would have seen these images as symbols of incompatible realities, I now saw no conflict. There was no meaningful distinction between the holy man chanting the name of God and the radio station logo to his left. No inner walls to touch, no outer walls to scale. It was *all* God's country. The lights of the city and the inner light of the holy man were spiritually synonymous.

This moment signaled a profound shift in consciousness. The light of the call now sifted even the grit of the marketplace through its sweet fingers. In a flash, I understood the primary reason why I had so often fled the culture to find God: I needed to get Buddhaland deep inside me before I could see it everywhere.

Intrinsic to my sense of unity was the subsequent disappearance of Little Missy. No sightings, no sensings, no trail of clues to lead me home. My precious sherpa had carried my soul-scriptures under her wings until I was ready to carry them. Now that I had become immovably lodged in my calling, she absorbed right back into me. Return to sender, address *now* known.

In serving me, Little Missy had been the consummate multi-tasker. She began her duties as a pied piper of Essence, playing her sweet soul flute at the most opportune moments. Then she was my in-house counsel, advocating for true-path until I was ready to speak for myself. Next, a courageous pilot flying me through the eye of the storm to the center of my being. At other times she was my gardener, planting and nourishing soul seeds when I was not looking. Finally, Little Missy was that rarest of salespersons, actually selling me on something I genuinely needed—true-path. It was a hard sell, but she persisted and closed the deal. A true renaissance woman, I bowed to her inventiveness. The little voice that knows….

While Little Missy faded, the Warrior actively returned into consciousness. Instead of being met with hostility, I now embraced him. He was not my enemy. He was essential to this journey of unfolding. Without his strength and fortitude, I could not have begun to refine the art of surrender.

I recognized that I had misunderstood the nature of soulshaping. Old soulshapes don't fade away. They just get pushed aside as the new forms come into being. When the new form concretizes, the old forms rise back into awareness. Where before the warrior and healer archetypes appeared to be flowing in disparate directions, they were now revealed as inextricable branches of the same waterway. On the river of Essence, everything flows in the same direction—toward the ocean of wholeness.

When Ego Has Landed

Arising from the sacred balance was a new relationship to my ego. For many years it felt more comfortable to attach to the proud armor of my individual achievements than surrender to my individual insignificance. Yet through a more unified lens, my ego started to lose its intense grip on my consciousness. It didn't mean that I had no ego, but rather that the ego was nestling into something bigger. It finally had some company.

Humbling toward ecstasy, I began to get it: I am but one student in the university of heart knocks. I have a relevant but limited role to play. I am the *doer* but I am also being *done* by something bigger. Only one question really matters: am I honoring my small part in the bigger ocean?

This experience helped me to resolve the seeming tension between Eastern and Western messages about the ego. Eastern Spirituality celebrates the dissipation of the ego, Western Psychology champions the strengthening and integration of the ego. As it turns out, they are both right. Once we have done enough work to establish our sense of self, we organically merge with the bigger ocean. It is not that we become less self-loving. We just merge our experience of self with something vaster than our individual achievements. We-self. The key is waiting until the ego is well-integrated and solid before diving in.

In this balanced state, I was soon reminded of the principles of connective-ness that had threaded through my journey. Again, we are all subscribers to the Universal Broadcasting System, that benevolent network of relatedness that brings lessons and messengers onto our path in an effort to grow us to the next stage of our expansion. Here the waves of serendipity are always lapping, although they go tidal when we align with spirit and jump into our deepest ocean. Here there are no coincidences, only summonings.

Now waves of serendipity began pouring in to support my unfolding. The first wave involved my business. One of my friends had worked for me for years, but he had always resisted the opportunity to run the business. He felt he wasn't ready for adult responsibility. A few months after I began to write, he met a hardworking, no-nonsense single mother. After little time with her, he became a father to her son and took over the day-to-day running of my business. This startling shift in him allowed me to honor my call more deeply. Without it, I would have been trying to write my first book forever.

Two years later, my dearest friend, my eighty-nine-year-old grand-mother, was sick in hospital. One morning I jumped out of bed very early to race to her side. I said, "I felt like you were summoning me." She said, "I was. Jeffrey, I think my number's up." No drama, just grounded Bubbi wisdom. I tried to encourage her, but she gave me the look. She said, "I'm tired of fighting. I'll always love you. I will walk beside you, in front of you, and above you every step of the way." She wanted permission to surrender. I gave it to her.

A few days later, I went to see her again. As she sat so vulnerable in her hospital bed, she gingerly reached for a newspaper article. Her nephew Jerry, a popular newspaper columnist, had been awarded a prize for journalism a few days earlier. Ever the lover of family, her eyes lit up. She did not know that he had died the night before.

As Jerry was being eulogized the next day, I saw myself at the pulpit eulogizing Bubbi. It felt imminent. After the service, I felt summoned away from the funeral procession. I left it and drove past her apartment. I couldn't look. I knew she was gone. I went to the office and checked my messages. She had died while I was driving to the funeral.

That night she reassured me. In the middle of the night I was awakened by the most horrible sound—a death cry, like nothing I have ever heard. I looked out the window. It was a foggy night, eerily foreboding. I saw a big raccoon dangling upside down on my tree, right in front of my bedroom window. The branch it was on was so thin, I didn't understand how the animal could hang from it without the branch breaking. This raccoon was doing everything in its power to get right side up so he could walk along the branch to safety. There was a second raccoon at the other end of the branch, screeching out to the other. It was unbelievable how much they longed to be together.

I went outside and walked up to the tree. I said something and then suddenly the upside-down raccoon miraculously turned right side up. It calmly walked along the branch, joined up with its partner, and together they strolled down the tree and across the street like reunited lovers. It was one of those experiences that you just know was intended for you.

My grandparents met on the street and they just knew that they were soul-mates. And after many decades of love their bodies separated, perhaps never to touch again. But when I saw those raccoons, I was sure that I didn't have to worry about my grandmother's passage. She was the upside-down raccoon, unwilling to get right side up and join her partner until I came outside and saw that she was going to be okay.

Weeks later, she let me know that she was watching over me. When my grandmother was in the hospital, she kept trying to give me fifteen hundred dollars toward my mortgage. It was her dying wish. A few weeks after she died, I told my mother—her executor—about it. She wasn't in a financial position to honor the wish. That next weekend, my mother went to the casino she often frequented with Bubbi and won fifteen hundred dollars. Is the bigger picture not obvious enough yet?

From Sole to Soul

After Bubbi died, my relationship to manifestation dramatically transformed. Whatever experience my soul needed for its expansion seemed to come through with fewer obstructions.

One day my friend suggested that I go to see Amma, the hugging saint, in Toronto. I was tired but remembered that Bhagavan Das had also told me to go see her. On the way I had the oddest feeling that I would meet a special woman there. The only other time I had felt that, I had met Rachel in Boulder.

Right after arriving, I saw an ex-girlfriend join the line-up. We were driven apart by odd circumstances, and we had unfinished business. I gave her my new number. She was the special one, maybe?

A woman walked hurriedly past and caught my eye. I left the building and walked across the parking lot. That same woman was now there, looking on the ground for her lost car key. I went over to help and her key appeared. She began to walk away, but I ran after her. I complimented her and offered my card. Sasha snapped it out of my hand like I had the plague.

I got involved with the ex-girlfriend. About eight weeks later, we had a phone conversation that ended our relationship for good. I got off the phone and went to the Internet cafe. Right in the heart of that conversation, Sasha had finally e-mailed me, two months after I'd met her. We spoke the next week. She had flown two thousand miles from her home in Alberta to get a birthday hug from Amma that night in Toronto. It turned out that I had actually met Sasha eight years earlier on her cousin's front porch, two doors down from my house in Toronto. Interestingly, she had been given her spiritual name by Baba Hari Dass, one of the gurus that Bhagavan Das studied with in India.

I spoke with Bhagavan Das about coming back to Toronto to chant. It was arranged and we agreed that he would stay with me. About a week before he came, a friend suggested that I make a documentary about him while he was here. While I was thinking about it, my neighbor came over with a book I just "had to read." The book? *Chant and Be Happy.* In ten years as neighbors, I had never heard her utter a single spiritual word.

As I waited to pick up Bhagavan Das at the airport, I hearkened back to the first time I saw him at Harbin seven years earlier. At that time I sensed that he was somehow part of my innate image. And as I saw him walk into the terminal, I knew that I was always going to make the film with him. It was in my soul-scriptures at (p)age 42 and three-quarters.

One afternoon I interviewed Mira Grof, a dear friend of Bhagavan Das. When I showed Sasha the footage, she recognized Mira as a stranger whom she had met that night at Amma's event. Sasha was about to leave when Mira encouraged her to stay until the morning chant. She stayed, and met me shortly thereafter. Clearly we all came together, if only for a moment, because there were gifts waiting to be opened.

Toward the end of the filming, my most significant gift revealed itself to me. Throughout my journey, I had wrestled with questions around the meaning of grounded spirituality: What does it mean to live a spiritual life? What would that actually look like? How does one live in God while living in a human body?

As I spent more time around "spiritual" people, I found myself getting more and more confused. There were spiritual seekers who looked for God in their minds, others who looked for her inside their bodies. Still others searched for her outside their bodies, on a pogo stick to the stars. It was all good, but was it all God?

Adding to my confusion were all the spiritualists who didn't seem to have any interest in dealing with their emotional pain, as though their issues were all an illusion. I was particularly compelled by the blissed-out ones, perhaps because I had the same tendency in myself. They were full of feeling, starry-eyed and positive, but something was not quite right.

Confusing me further were spiritualists with obvious integrity issues. I met them at the retreat centers and yoga studios, and in Sasha's stories about gurus and their disillusioned disciples. They seemed to imagine enlightenment as something distinct from morality. Anything goes in the quest for God. Yet it seemed to me that if you were truly enlightened, all of your chakras (energy centers) would be healthy and unobstructed. With your heart chakra open, you would naturally care about others and behave with integrity, right?

I asked several seekers how to reconcile immorality with heightened consciousness. In other words, can an immoral person become enlightened? Many of them said that there was no relationship between morality and God-realization. Realization comes to whomever it comes to. Interesting.

I meditated on this for a while, and then I understood. What they were talking about was a different kind of spirituality than the one I was interested in. They were after the enlightenment moment. I was after the enlightened way of being. They were grasping for God rather than rising up to meet her. On their model, you may well have peak experiences, but you will not be able to sustain them. You will inevitably fall back down to the level of your unresolveds.

Now I knew what grounded spirituality wasn't. But what was it?

The answer came to me in the form of Ram Dass, the author of *Be Here Now*. Led to the feet of his guru by Bhagavan Das, Ram Dass was instrumental in bringing Eastern spirituality to the West. I had the privilege of interviewing him for the Bhagavan Das documentary at Ram Dass's home in Maui. Although he had suffered a serious stroke years before, he showed up with his soul a-blazin' and gave us everything he had over parts of two days. To think, I complain when I have to eat airplane food, or don't get enough time to myself.

As the interviews progressed, I noticed how different my experience of spirituality was in his presence. Where other spiritual teachers often seemed to take me out of my body, I felt more deeply in my body near Ram Dass. I could really *feel* him and the inextricable link between the emotional body and the spirit. There was my beating heart, there were the tears in my eyes, and there was God. And it was all the same.

There was this subtle, magnificent moment. Ram Dass was sitting in his wheelchair, quietly looking out the window at the birds drinking water on the rear porch. His eyes were moist and tender. Such a simple thing, yet everything was there—God watching God drinking God. All one.

In *Still Here,* Ram Dass wrote that he had spent most of his life keeping his awareness free of his body, ignoring his body, pushing it away. But the stroke had changed all of that. It grounded him and brought him back into connection with his body. He calls this stroke of good luck *Fierce Grace*. In his words, "I came to appreciate that, however wonderful it is as a practice, 'I am not this body' is only half the truth. The stroke brought me squarely in touch with the fact that, although I certainly am *more* than my body, I also *am* this body."

Near him, I got what was missing for me with some of the other teachers I had encountered. There is something very beautiful about their hunger for God, but there is something frightening about a spiritual intention not grounded in the earthly realms. It is the unrooted trip-out rather than the solidly rooted trip-in, a form of openness that is not actually open, because there is no structure to ground it.

On the flight home my philosophy of grounded spirituality began to concretize. I call it *Ascending with Both Feet on the Ground*. It is the idea that our ascension to heightened consciousness can only be sustained if it is an embodied unfolding from the ground up. We begin with the root chakra—the quest for *Om* begins at home—and we work our way up from there. It is not enough for our feet to merely skim the ground. The mythic life begins with our feet planted on Mother Earth. With our soles firmly planted, our soul has a leg to stand on in its efforts to go higher. From sole to soul....

At each subsequent stage of our ascension, we must deal with all the significant issues and lessons that obstruct us. Our spiritual ascension is intrinsically linked to our capacity to live in and through *all* aspects of reality: shadow and light, earth and sky, grocery list and unity consciousness. This is in the courageous and inclusive nature of "enrealment."

Once we have learned our lessons and cleared enough space inside, we are truly present in our body. From this presence emerges a natural and sustainable movement upward, toward God. Inner meets outer on a well-fortified bridge of golden light. Alexander Lowen put it beautifully: "Sensing the harmony between the internal pulsation of our body and that in the universe, we feel identified with the universal, with God. We are like two tuning forks vibrating to the same pitch."

Of course, this view of ascension is very different from the spiritual bypass approach. The bypasser looks outside the body for spirituality rather than in the heart of it. He turns to God reactively, in a determined effort to get away from here. The deeper ocean feels safer than the riptides of disappointment and grief on Mother Earth. I think of it as the difference between someone who looks to the skies while standing on stilts and one who looks with their feet planted firmly on the ground. Like a one-winged bird, the stilt walker will eventually come crashing down to earth.

To ascend, we must bridge one wing—the Eastern quest for the eternal—with the other wing—the Western quest for emotional health. Get in your body. Heal yourself. Open your heart. Ascend to God.

Homeward Unbound

Toward the end of this writing, I summoned a number of challenges into my life. The first was the loss of my friend as the ground for my business. His attempts at adult responsibility lasted four years before his self-destructive patterns got the best of him.

While I was deep into the second draft, I found out that he had been stealing sales leads for months to support his drug habit. He had also stolen thousands of dollars from installations. By the time he got caught, he had put me into tremendous debt. Sadly, I had to fire him. But my faith passed another test. I continued to write despite the profound economic pressure and feelings of betrayal.

Then the next challenge. The installer who replaced him was almost killed in a highway accident while on his way to work. A few weeks later, the secretary who ran my office lost her voice because of a tumor in her throat. I was being severely tested by the Universal Broadcasting System.

While sitting at the computer one night, I could swear that some of my dead relatives were gathered around me, willing me onward. For the next two weeks, we were inseparable. I pushed on through; they pushed me harder. In their presence, I recognized how significant this moment was for all of us.

In a survivalist world, it is rare for anyone to even identify his or her calling. Most of us barely ever scratch the itch. When you have the chance to actualize them, you have to try, because you are not doing it for yourself alone. You are also doing it for all the members of your soulpod. If you complete your task, however small or humble it may be, you take them all to the next level.

In the last chapter of the book, I inwardly dedicated each paragraph to a different family member. I wrote for my sister Robin, who died after only a few days, her callings never to see the light of day. I wrote for Uncle Al, stuck on a hospital gurney with heart disease for much of his adult life. I wrote for my grandparents, whose greatest gift was to give all the love that they had to a little boy, so he could one day fly. I wrote a paragraph for cousin Gloria, living in a nursing home, prevented by some odd twist of fate from honoring her highest heartfelt intentions. I wrote for my Dad, the best writer in the family, who has risen above his childhood circumstances in ways that I cannot even imagine. And I wrote for Auntie Ova, beaten down by a difficult husband, whose great gift was warm chocolate pudding that restored your faith in God.

I was overcome with gratitude for all of them. How could I have gotten to this point without them? If my great-grandparents hadn't overcome the odds and moved to Canada, where would I be? If my grandparents hadn't given me the love that I didn't get at home, would I even be alive today? The simple fact that they had come before gave me some form of structure to support my movement upward. *Glory to those who came before.*

My web of gratitude has spread to the culture itself. Western culture has its problems, but it is also far ahead of most of the world with respect to basic rights and freedoms. Here I was afforded the opportunity to pull myself out of the kind of poverty that is seldom overcome in the developing world. Here I could build a business that afforded me the opportunity to adventure beyond my limited geography and explore other ways of being. Here I was able to satisfy a preliminary need for sturdiness before seeking out more subtle satisfactions.

I often experience myself ascending with both feet on the ground. I feel solidly rooted, and feather-light—a bare-able lightness of being. I pay my mortgage and I also pay the karmic upkeep on my spiritual home. Karmic currency includes benevolent acts, actualized callings, prayerful moments. The purer our intention, the greater the return.

I had always believed that sensitivity is impossible to hold to in a harsh world. Yet in this moment, I feel sensitive, but without the fragility. My soulshape has expanded to accommodate my vulnerability and strength at the same time. Gracegrit.

Sometimes I feel like I touch into a way of being that transcends or subsumes gender. It is a way of being that is Essence-identified. Neither man nor woman, *I am soul*.

I am also experiencing many aspects of my life as a daily spiritual practice, where my way of being flows straight from my spiritual center. This involves seeing and being spirit everywhere—in the ways I eat (devotional), interact (namaste), walk (eye on the heavens, feet on the ground), and in the grateful and gracious manner I touch myself and my loved ones.

My heart itself is finally open. My connection to God roars through my open heart. Closing the heart is a self-fulfilling prophecy. When we close it, we attract more reasons to keep it closed. Opening the heart is a soul-fulfilling prophecy. When we open it, we attract blessings—open bless-a-me! Finally blessings have a way in, and a way out to touch others. The key to it all was listening to the little voice that knows. Although it came through in hints and whispers, it had an odd sense of authority to it. A distant flute with the energy of a symphony. Only now do I realize how much mine loved me. Had I bypassed it, I would be suffering horribly right now. I would be practicing law day and night. I would probably be married to someone who didn't touch my core. If I was real lucky, my soul would still be grumbling, and the universe would still be trying to trip me *up*. But who knows? Ten years on false-path can numb the strongest of callings.

Now and then I remember what it felt like to drive with my family through the streets of Toronto. Driving down Bathurst Street in our Pontiac Prison, it seemed absolutely impossible to imagine a profound life. Everything felt so completely bleak. Though I appreciate that people have overcome far worse circumstances, the simple fact that I have moved from that place of embedded despair to this moment of hope tells me that most anyone can create a better life if they put their spirits to it.

No matter how bad life got, I always felt some dissonance with the bleaksters and their mantras of meaninglessness: "Thank God it's Friday," "Life's a bitch and then you die." Somewhere deep inside I had a little trickle of faith that there was something purposeful happening here. You have to believe that or you won't do the work. Faith is the elixir that gets you back on the path when you can't walk another step.

With my expansion has come a genuine sense of liberation. No longer at risk of being buried in the tomb of the unknown souldier, I feel liberated from doubt and confusion. I feel liberated from that overwhelming longing for he who waits on the other side. I know why I am here. I know *who* I am here.

This liberation manifests by a certain glow—a *soul sheen*—that I carry around with me wherever I go, keeping me warm on dark winter nights. My body is streaming with energy, and it is a purer bead of energy because it is authentically sourced. This confirms that the body really is the mill for the soul's journey. It declines when it is alienated from its essential path, and it sparkles with life while walking it.

When the deeper ocean fades from view, I know that it means that my body masks have returned. I try not to keep them up for too long. Back to the massage table, or the yoga mat, or the hitting cube. Whatever it takes to peel the armor and open the channel. I am particularly drawn to subtle techniques like watsu (water shiatsu) and cranial-sacral massage. These approaches seem to speak to and from the soul-self, inviting the body to soften from the inside out.

While there is more peace, I am by no means joyous all the time. Although they say that "the joy is in the journey," I didn't find it so much joyous as progressively more real. It got more real the farther I went, and that meant a deeper experience of both joy and suffering. To be sure, I am better able to derive meaning from my suffering, but it still hurts like hell.

Although many of my wounds have gone quieter, I am still challenged by certain ones that won't go away. My abandonment wound in particular does not want to die. And I am still a charter member of Do-aholics Anonymous. I do too much, and this pattern sometimes keeps me from fully surrendering to the moment.

As part of the journey, I may have to accept that certain wounds will never fade altogether. It does not all come out in the wash. Just when you think the monster has died, he shows up on your doorstep begging to see you. Perhaps healing is not always about killing him when he comes. Perhaps it is also about learning how to move forward despite him.

Although I have proudly earned a BA degree in—what shall we call it, interior design?—I am often reminded that I have much more coursework left to do. There are so many new lessons waiting at the gate, further opportunities to expand my soul into the next shape in its evolution.

As it turns out, life really isn't a dress rehearsal. It's an *undress rehearsal.* We come down here time and time again to practice shedding our ego armor until we can step on the stage of eternity, naked and exposed before God, as God. *Exit, cloud left.*

May you have the courage to remove your armor and bare yourself before your truth, time and time again. May you shape your soul a little bit more with every breath. The gift of eternal life longs to be opened.

Souldendum

Final Thoughts on the Path from a Seasoned Inner-War Veteran

Soulshaping invites us to become responsible for our own life and to live it authentically. It asks us to make a distinction between a timely and a timeless way of being. At the heart of small mind is the tendency to see the world in timely terms—trends, worldliness, the opinions of others. At the heart of big mind is an emphasis on timeless considerations—the bigger picture, archetypal rhythms, purpose and meaning. Although they are inextricably linked, it is helpful to distinguish our deeper reasons for being from the motivations engendered by the culture. Strive to reach the stage where your most significant choices and actions are emanating from the soul outward, uninfluenced by the world at large.

No Delay

Everywhere I look I see people who are walking a false path. Their obsession with "security" at the expense of their callings compels them to do jobs they hate. Grin and bear it, until I turn sixty-five, and then my real life will begin. What if our soul-scriptures only give us fifty years to actualize them?

By the time we retire at sixty-five many of us cannot even begin to access our real self. With our God-seeds planted in the wrong fields, we have become too tired and even ill from carrying the weight of the lie to really touch the moment. Forty years encased in stone will do that to you. And that's if we survive until then—many of us die from the lie. If we don't shape *up*, we may be shipped out.

If we do what we really love, there is no such thing as retirement. The soul beat goes on. If we love our work, we may well make less money before sixty-five, but we are much more likely to live longer and healthier, and to actually want to work well past sixty-five. Is wholeness not the only retirement plan worth saving for?

Somehow it all comes down to truth, or consequences. There is something seemingly safe about living falsely. On one level everything remains unreal, even suffering, because we are walking a false path. Our choices are holdbacks, hiding places, escape hatches. If we don't get what we want, we don't really care. It wasn't our *real* path anyway.

But the consequences of our falsity are profound. When we live our truth, there is no dissonance along the mind-body-spirit continuum. We flow in the river true. Yet when we lie to ourselves, we corrupt our inner world. It takes an enormous amount of energy to self-distort. The lies get into our cells, and we suffer for it. The convenient fictions we tell ourselves to keep the truth at bay — "I'll live my truth later ... after I pay off the house" — become inconvenient factions that congeal and ultimately undermine our very existence. We should be more afraid of avoiding our path than living it.

If thinking of our own death doesn't motivate us, it may help to think of those who never made it down the birth canal. Think of those little ones who tasted but a few breaths before succumbing. Think of those who died on battlefields so that we would have a chance to be free. Remember how hard they fought for this life, how badly they wanted it.

No matter what others have mistakenly told us, we are all needed here for our gifts, however small or humble they may outwardly appear. If not, the universe would take us back in the blink of an eye. No matter what we may have done in our lifetime, no matter how uncomfortable we are with our past actions, there is always the chance of growing our soul a little bit more.

Dear Reader, please walk your own way while you still can. The truth is that there is no escape from reality. There is only postponement. When it comes down to it — and make no mistake, it *does* come down to it — all you are is your soul's journey. What else is there? What else is worthy of the time that you have been given?

Shtuscle and Flow

Soulshaping is very much the artist's journey. Our inner world is soul art; our lives its canvas. Like true artists, we have to be both willful and surrendered at the same time. We have to allow our form to change as intuition demands. Home is where the art is.

Let there be no doubt, this is no easy creation in a challenged world. The world is still a care-less place. Heartfelt glimpses of the God within are discarded as corny and impractical (pray to schmaltz!). Brief crack-opens get glued over for fear that everything that holds us together will come unglued (let it unglue!). Interactions with like-spirited others that hint of the deeper ocean get misplaced, buried below the weight of survivalism and distraction (rise from the shallows!).

To craft the truest image, we need to make soul-tracking fundamental to our daily consciousness. And we need to develop and utilize our inner tools. The most important tool is *shtuscle*—inner muscle, the soul-driven determination to overcome whatever obstacles come our way. Without shtuscle, and lots of it, we're not getting home.

At the heart of the challenge is the courage to be vulnerable. Although the world rewards insensitivity with the spoils of war, it takes more courage to surrender than to numb. So often the most damaged people are the most advanced and feeling souls. They feel everything and are more strongly impacted by the disparity between an authentic life and the falsified energy of the world. We have to never surrender our right to surrender.

It is good to be patient with ourselves on this journey. Growers are inchworms. Transforming the shape of the soul is a lifelong process. Profound experiences can accelerate the journey, but much of the real change happens at slower paces and the places in between. It also helps to "soulebrate" our little victories along the way rather than waiting until we reach some illusory perfection. Although the journey can be difficult, there is something wonderfully gratifying about the processes of change. A new set of eyes each stage, a new soul-skin at every turn. What an honor and a wonder to self-create.

To achieve the greatest clarity, it is essential to construct a spacious and flowing inner world—if you build it, *you* will come! Without breathing room inside the body temple, it can be difficult to identify our soul-scriptures. Triggered by old material, we expend all our energy putting out internal fires instead of channeling it to higher considerations.

Creating space is often a question of clearing emotional debris. I cannot overstate the importance of doing this work as part of the spiritual journey. Divesting ourselves of our emotional holdings is the greatest investment in our future. Remember, we don't need to get everything in place before we move our feelings. In fact, we may need to move them before we can get everything in place. Things come a lot easier when there is more space inside.

At the same time, we have to be very gentle with the ways we protect ourselves. Our defenses were the third arm that appeared at the most opportune moment, just as we were about to fall into suffering. Severing them with harshness only keeps the suffering that birthed them alive. As Mark Twain said, "Habit is habit, and not to be flung out of the window by any man, but coaxed downstairs one step at a time."

Be conscious of the role that gender conditioning may play in holding you back. For example, many men were conditioned to be rigid and focused. The very thing they need to grow—a heartlong plunge into their own confusion—is internally unacceptable. Also, many men were trained not to be profoundly vulnerable in relationship. Yet many of our soul's lessons come through connection. Similarly, many women were conditioned to live everything through relationship. Yet many of our soul's lessons demand that we walk the path of the lone wolf from time to time.

A final word on shame: If there is any one thing that can hold us back, it is our own self-loathing. If we move through our lives ashamed of ourselves, it is very difficult to imagine and believe in our highest possibilities. Unfortunately we often don't know how much shame we carry. Droplets of shame get behind our eyes and blind us to who we really are.

We need to get to know our shame. We need to track it and understand its insidious impact on our inner life. And we need to help one another to bring it into the light. We need to share those things that we are ashamed of with each other, thereby freeing ourselves and giving others permission to be liberated as well. Self-admission is the first step on the road to self-acceptance. Every deep dark secret we hide is fundamentally human. How can it be any other way?

Shame is rooted in the shame pit of generations before, perpetuating the self-hatred of the collective unconscious, still lodged in dark energies and imaginings. Your shame has nothing to say about who you really are, never did, never will. In truth, you don't need anyone else's permission to show yourself. God gave you all the permission you need.

A Good Psychotherapist Never Hurts

To accelerate our healing, it is often useful to work with a psychotherapist. Be careful with your choice. The relationship between client and therapist can profoundly impact the healing process. You want to find a therapist whom you feel a genuine resonance with. When you first meet them, see it as an interview. Ask questions about their own journey: What is their core healing philosophy? What called them to this work? What issues have they struggled with? How far have they come on their journey? How far do they still have to go?

All too often, clients don't move forward in therapy because they are working with a stuck therapist. Therapists are essentially tour guides. They can only take you through terrain that they themselves have walked. For instance, if a therapist has not reached a place of personal joy, they may keep you over-identified with your pain.

In the same way, be careful that your therapist is not perpetuating your own victimization. A good therapist invites you to accept and express your victimization, and then guides you to a place of self-responsibility, where you can take adult responsibility for your future actions. I have seen many clients stuck in the victim mode by therapists who are themselves stuck there.

The good therapist also understands the difference between guiding and taking over. Telling the other what I think happened to them sets up a disempowering dynamic. I become the parent and they remain as children, directed and defined by the omnipotent other. You want a therapist who takes over only when necessary.

A word about mainstream psychiatrists. They are the perfect people to visit if your only hope is medication. But if there is still a chance that you can be healed (and there almost always is), stay away from them if at all possible. In many cases, they are more analytic than therapeutic. Knowing *why* you do something is not enough to heal you.

With respect to psychotropic medications, it is good to be cautious when we walk down this road. Many of those medications are feeling-stuffers. They deaden the system and block its natural flow. All the held emotions that want to thaw and move out of us get blocked at their source. All the new life experiences with the potential for creating new associations cannot get inside. We have to be emotionally liquid before we can flow.

In the same way, be careful with the labels psychiatrists use. For example, calling someone a "manic depressive" often shifts the focus from a psycho-emotional experience to a categorical description. Instead of focusing on the source spring—Why does the client go manic when she feels her pain? What pain is she trying to get away from?—the label invites the psychiatrist to take the client on the drug trip. There is a fine line between stabilizing someone for therapeutic purposes and embedding their pattern further.

In addition, most psychiatrists (and many other psychology "professionals") do not understand the relationship between the body and the psyche. For example, when they look at "projection," they only look at it as a habit of mind. But projection is a body defense as well. As spiritual intuitive Abraham noted, "When we contract, we project." Projection emanates from and directly reflects a fearful, contracted emotional body. If we do not address the emotional body itself, there is very little chance of healing our defensive patterns. For this reason, a good body-centered psychotherapist can make all the difference.

Turning the Soulular Phone On

As space opens up inside, we often turn our attention to identifying our callings. To help us with this, it is essential that we spend a lot of time inside. So much of soulshaping is about the subtleties of inner design. Inside is where we separate the gold from the dross. Inside is where we do the work to uncover our original face. We have to sit down inside ourselves often and do our inner homework. When man walked on the moon, we attuned to every step with bated breath. Now bring the same focus inward and pay exquisite attention to your inner steps.

At other times, it is good to adventure outward and explore new possibilities. Call them depth charges, call them crack-opens, call them shots in the arm. Like swashbucklers of the spirit, we bravely seek out any experience that might inform our path. When we are afraid of something, we live it fully and see what floats to the surface in the doing. We participate in our own revealing.

I want to really emphasize the value of retreats and workshops, particularly those held away from home. Because we are often adapted to our roles in our daily life, it is difficult to try new ways of being on for size. On retreat we have a wonderful opportunity to let go of our local framework of perception and adventure into broader realms of possibility.

Soulshaping also means not being afraid to do things that feel weird—*weird your way to God.* There can be something very helpful about doing things that feel strangely unlike who we think we are. Many of the things we resist contain the seeds of our unfolding.

It is also important to keep the quest for Essence alive. Even an occasional dip in its pools will expand our soul's consciousness. It is like gazing at the valley from the top of the mountain instead of the bottom. We see more than just a few localized trees and a small part of the river. We see the bigger picture. The monkey mind feeds on "small peanuts": tireless anxieties, petty jealousies, fearful imaginings. Starve it by swimming in a vast ocean of delight.

If we swim here often enough, we won't need harshness to wake us up. We will already be awake. There will still be suffering, but it will not be as malicious in its intention. Now we learn from sweeter experiences: the change of a season, the touch of a cat, and the old friend that we bump into right after thinking about her. We enter a more subtle and sophisticated understanding of God's world.

Do not be dissuaded if your call begins quietly. It may be in hiding, but it's still in there, still breathing, still with a soulbeat. When the soulular phone finally rings, answer it! It's the divine Mother calling to remind you of why you are here. You are one of the lucky ones. Most never hear it ring.

God is IN the People

At the heart of Soulshaping is a profound faith in the human experience, in the karmic significance of our personal identity. This stands in real contrast to some of the detachment models that are gaining favor in Western culture. These models present true-path as something distinct from the emotional body, as though our usual self-identifications are inherently inauthentic, as though our physical forms are inferior. At the extremes, they seem to suggest that God made a mistake when she placed us in human bodies. These models worry me and present an image of heightened consciousness that often feels more robotic than human, more heady than hearty.

Soulshaping is not a detachment model. It is an immersion model. It is about jumping into life, immersing ourselves in our feelings and experiences in an effort to learn what we need to expand our soul's consciousness. It is about "feeling" God, not "thinking" God. It is about honoring our personal identity and our physical form as not only the "vessel" for the soul, but as the embodiment of the soul as well. Embodied spirituality.

To be sure, there are times when detachment is necessary: when the suffering is too much, when we need a peek into a vaster reality. Indeed we are far more than our monkey mind, our neurotic attachments, our linear lens. But to live in perpetual detachment is to miss the moment altogether. It is to trip out of the body that carries the karmic seeds for our transformation. It is to leave Earth before our time.

The most inclusive answer is to work on eradicating our misguided notions of "I" until our notions of I-ness become directly linked to who we *really* are, to a conscious awareness of our soul-scriptures for this lifetime. To do this we may have to become initially effective at detachment techniques. But then, when we are ready, we come back down to Earth and work with what lives inside us. This means learning how to cultivate our bodies as gardens of truth. This means calling ourselves on our detachment from our shadow. This means doing the often-difficult work to clear our emotional debris and gain control over our relational patterns. We clear our emotional debris because it creates space inside for our authentic self to emerge, and also because inherent in those feelings and memories are the lessons we need to grow in our spirituality. Our thoughts are only illusions when they do not reflect who we really are, our emotions only wasteful when we are not seeing them all the way through to the spiritual lessons they contain. When we are aligned with our authenticity, our feelings and thoughts become instruments of true-path, direct expressions of our highest intentions. In this more authentic state, we become much more effective at attracting what we want from a universe that is only interested in authentic expansion. Nothing feigned will do.

Our humanness is the "I" of the soul needle. It is our soul clay. It is the heart of our magnificence. God is in our humanness, God is in our connectiveness, God is in our broken hearts, God is *in* the people. I-God.

A Warning about Gurus

Some of us turn to gurus to help us home. In the Hindu tradition, a distinction is made between two types: (1) sat-guru, and (2) upa-guru. A sat-guru is a realized master. She is the way. Amma and Neeb Karori Baba are said to be examples of sat-guru. An upa-guru is a door opener. They influence a shift in your consciousness. They show you some part of the way. Anyone—your mother, your cat, the homeless guy who tells you to get out of your head—can be an upa-guru.

When someone presents themselves as a sat-guru, or when we project sat-guru onto someone, we tread on dangerous ground. To be sure, some individuals are worthy of our devotion, but we have to be very careful. The legacy of the exploitative guru is a long one, and it has caused undue suffering.

There are many signs that we are dealing with an ungrounded and potentially untrustworthy spiritual teacher. For instance, they have one set of rules for you, one for them. They deny their unresolved issues. They see the body as substandard or entirely distinct from the soul. They reframe painful life experiences *only* in terms of spiritual learning. They see the world of emotions as illusion (except when it is convenient not to). They rely on their so-called *purity* as an excuse for not forming adult boundaries. They defend their behavior by reference to a higher knowing. If you complain about their actions, you are told that your complaints are emanating from the mundane world and that you just can't grasp their lens. They may also re-frame their own dysfunction in heightened terms ("I quit the world because I had a higher calling") rather than facing their shadow head-on ("I had too many issues to deal with the world"). A giant warning sign is the use of "the mirror" as a defense against wrongdoing. The guru claims that his (questionable) actions were not actually for his own benefit but done with the conscious intention of reflecting back to you the unresolved aspects of your own consciousness. If you felt betrayed, it was because you have issues around betrayal that you need to look at.

If we do choose to sit before someone, grounded spirituality demands that we check in as to our motivation. If we are lost in the perfection projection, we need to own that. If we are looking for the good father or mother, we need to own that too. In most cases, the guru is just a travel agent for the particular trip that helped him to become more aligned. With only rare exceptions, he cannot tell us our truth. He cannot tell us what to know. The most he can do is call out to our knowing and remind us of what we inherently knew all along. Anything else is usually a misappropriation of karmic funds. Be careful.

If we just see everyone as an upa-guru, then we can avoid many of the pitfalls that come with the sat-guru projection. Better yet, chase ourselves down the way we chase down the guru. See our own lives as guru. Sit before it as student and teacher. What a thing—to be teacher and student both!

A Soulful World

In my imaginings, I see a world that makes the journey of the soul its most important priority. Here, we adjust every aspect of our lives to its authority. If a forty-hour work week takes us out of attunement, we change the work week. If too much stimulation alienates us from the source spring, we consciously limit it. If fifteen hugs per day keep us connected, we insist on them. Our environment and our terms of reference are shaped from the soul outward.

In this soulful world, we would pay homage to the steps that we have taken to find our way home. We would honor the same in others, recognizing the courage it took to live in truth. People often talk about living in the moment, but it is my experience that we do not live in the moment if we are not living in truth. **TRUTH IS THE GATEWAY TO THE MOMENT.** It doesn't matter how much we achieve, or how many things we master, if it is not our true-path. The moment we lie, we leave the moment. The work we do to separate false-path from true-path is not just spiritually beneficial, it is our best and only hope.

Lately, I have been imagining an international holiday called "True-Path Day." We have holidays to celebrate our battles for outer freedom, but few that acknowledge our fight for inner freedom. On True-Path Day, we would soulebrate every effort we have made to excavate and embody the soul-scriptures that live at the core of our being. Every calling that was explored and every essential lesson that we learned would be held and seen in its highest light. The ramifications of such a day would be profound, particularly for the younger soulshapers. Instead of being conditioned to play it safe, they would be encouraged to live in truth as a way of being. Later in life, when the little voice pipes up in their inner world, they would happily raise it to the rafters of consciousness.

In this more liberated world, we would be easier on each other. We would always strive to see others as souls, even those we profoundly dislike. We would recognize that each of us is a soul at a particular stage in its development. The most we can do is inch a little forward each lifetime. Even those of us who are able to make giant leaps are still limited by the developmental stages of the collective unconscious. We can only jump so far before the world around us limits our expansion. We are all in this together. We *are* this together.

My favorite dream is that of a soulshaping university. *Soulshaping U* is dedicated to the opening of the heart and the excavation of our soul-scriptures from the library within. Courses are experiential in nature and might include Depth Charges; Ego Shucking; Emotional Clearing and Integration; Money Management; De-armoring; Dream Interpretation; Methods for Shedding Falsity; Issue Spotting; Meditation; Shazam: The Inner Wow-Wow! Because only the individual soul can know how close it is to true-path, the individual gives her own grades: Did I courageously depth-charge? Did I soul-attune, or did I soul-distract?

In addition to honoring the PhDs of the outer world, we would also honor those inner world guides who help us to shape our own myths.

In this soulful world, there would be a profound emphasis on relationship as a path to God. We would place much less emphasis on gender, and more emphasis on the spiritual threads that bring us together. We would be encouraged to summon and identify members of our soulpod from an early age.

There would also be a strong cultural emphasis on foundation building, recognizing that we cannot hold soul love safe until we have worked through our own obstacles to intimacy. You can't love another person if you can't see them, and you can't see them until you have clarified your own lens. At the same time, we would be under no illusion that all "soul-mates" are meant to last a lifetime. Some soul connections are meant to last but a moment. Whatever you need to smooth the rough edges of your soul.

In this love-struck world, relationship would always be experienced as spiritual practice, a devotional expression of our God-self. We would all be taught to recognize those who had encountered soul love, and we would support the related processes. Rather than blindly characterizing the tumult as pathology, we would accept that the tumult is often necessary, and sometimes quite beautiful.

To stay awake to the sacredness, relationship rituals would be taught and practiced everywhere. Fewer would get up on Saturday and Sunday mornings and go to houses of worship to come to God. Many would stay in bed on those mornings, turn to their partners, and come to God in their own houses of worship. Employees would get time off from work not just because they are physically ill but also because they need to tend to an unhealthy relationship. Couples would go on regular retreat where they would be fed and housed, and where elders would be present to help them through difficult moments. We would structure our world and define our values so that love can stay at the heart of the matter in every moment.

Help Wanted!

Soulshaping (Un)limited seeks like-spirited others to join a profound and tireless revolution of the spirit. Without your participation, our world of glorious possibility is at risk.

Joining begins within. There is no job interview, no grand inquisition. You look inside and decide if you are willing to do the work to excavate and honor your innate image for this lifetime. Only you will know if you have that willingness. If you do, get to work on whatever it is that stands between the you of this moment, and the *truest* you.

At some point, you may feel ready to bring your soul energy outward. You may want to gift back. In Sanskrit, the word *seva* means to be of service. How can you help "seva" this mad world? That is for you to decide. It can be as obvious as honoring your callings. It can be as subtle as attempting more genuine contact with others—"How are you? No, I mean how are you, really?" It doesn't matter what form it takes, so long as it feels true to path.

If the revolution can really gain steam, we will need all manner of soul workers and spiritual activists—unmaskers, initiators, excavators, humanifestors, lesson interpreters, energy workers, dream weavers, mystery mamas, handholders, ego-shuckers, boundary-makers, authenticators, guru busters, soulular phone operators, conscious flakes, masters of the heart. Whatever you have to overcome on the way home will prepare you to help others with the same challenges. I'll see you on the path....

Soulshaping Dictionary
TERMS OF (HE)ART

Ascending with both feet on the ground: Soulshaping is a philosophy of grounded spirituality. We grow by coming down into our body and our personhood and learning the lessons necessary for our expansion ("You have to grow down to grow up"). Ascending with both feet on the ground is the idea that our ascension to a more heightened consciousness can only be sustained if it is an embodied unfolding from the ground up (from Sole to Soul ...). We begin with the root chakra—the quest for *Om* begins at home—and we work our way up from there. It is not enough for our feet to merely skim the ground. The mythic life begins with our feet planted on Mother Earth. With our soles firmly planted, our soul has a leg to stand on in its efforts to go higher. Once the root chakra is satisfied, we proceed to the next chakras. As we heal, there emerges a natural and sustainable movement upward, toward God. This philosophy bridges the Eastern quest for the eternal with the Western quest for emotional health.

Authentications: Intentional efforts to authenticate those pathways that have called us. When the soulular phone rings, we answer the call by trying it on for size. As we explore it, we check its authenticity against our soul-scriptures to see if it is true to form.

Body masks: The physical armor we wear in order to adapt to and protect ourselves from various realities. Can come in countless forms such as shallow breath, rigid musculature, limited range of motion. To be distinguished from a state of embodiment that more directly reflects our essential self.

Callings: The particular form that our entelechy is here to take in this lifetime, the gifts we are here to humanifest. It can be as complex as finding the cure for cancer, as simple as learning how to listen. *Only soul knows* the path it is here to walk.

Cell your soul: The idea that the body is the karmic field where the soul's lessons are harvested (God is *IN* the people). In order to grow spiritually, we must bring our suffering and our joy through the cells of the body until our spiritual lessons are birthed. Repressed emotions are un-actualized spiritual lessons. To grow, we have to see our feelings all the way through. Once they make it all the way through the conversion tunnel, the lesson is revealed and the soul evolves to the next stage. Divine Perspiration.

Conscious adaptation: The idea that we choose all our adaptations (and disguises) with awareness, for a limited time and clearly defined purpose. We know who we really are, we know what masks to put on to deal with the circumstances before us, and we consciously remove them as soon as reasonably possible. Conscious armoring is one aspect of this.

Depth-avoidant behavior: Any behavior done with the intention of avoiding our true self and authentic experience.

Depth charges: In the context of psychological issues, depth charges are actions taken with the intention of triggering unacknowledged issues and repressed emotions into awareness. In the context of spiritual path, depth charges are intentional efforts to ignite our inner knowing and excavate our soul-scriptures from below the surface of our daily lives. Depth charges can take many forms, some radical and intense, some subtle and gentle.

Enrealment: The idea that a more "heightened" consciousness is not all about the light (as enlightenment implies) but is about becoming more real, more genuinely here in all respects—shadow and light, earth and sky, grocery list and unity consciousness. At the heart of *Enrealment* is the quest for a more inclusive consciousness, an attempt to live in all aspects of reality simultaneously rather than only those realms that feel the most comfortable. By living in the real, our experience of the moment is more complete, our ascension more true. *Be Real Now.*

Entelechy: The pre-encoded being we came here to manifest, and the tools we brought with us to manifest it. Actualizing our entelechy is the essence of our expansion. See also *Innate image.*

Essence-centered way of being: A way of being that is soul-driven. We make our choices as to path by listening in and tracking our soul's voice. Success is defined through the eyes of the soul—lessons, callings, authentic expansion. The ego is not our ruler anymore.

False-path: Any path that is not true to our entelechy in this lifetime. The sense that we are walking in someone else's shoes and not our own.

Forgiveness bypass: The tendency to avoid unresolved emotions by feigning forgiveness. Premature forgiveness.

Habitual range of e-motion: Our emotional comfort zone. The familiar place between armor and vulnerability that we come back to time and time again. Our expansion depends on our willingness to move beyond our habitual range.

Innate image: A term noted by James Hillman in *The Soul's Code*. In the context of *Soulshaping*, the innate image is a tangible representation of the soulshape we came here to embody. It is the being we are here to become. See also *Entelechy*.

Inner daimon: The presence that accompanies us on our life journey with the intention of reminding us of our true-path. This presence whispers sweet somethings in our ear, and even trips us up when necessary, in its determined efforts to bring us to the feet of our innate image. Also referred to as guiding angel, genius, deity, higher self, white shadow, and guiding light.

JAB: The Jealousy, Abandonment, and Betrayal emotional trigger. A powerful and often unhealed wound area that obstructs many individuals who are attempting to move forward on the path.

The Law of Averse Possession: The idea that we assume ownership of someone else's emotional material if we hold on to it for too long. When someone takes their stuff out on us, it moves from them to us. It remains ours until we choose to give it back, to express rather than repress the feelings that arise from the experience(s).

A leap of fate: A (courageous) jump onto the growing edge of our soul. A stepping out into our innate image.

The (real) Learning Channel: The channel that shows us the experiences and lessons that our soul chose for this lifetime. When we watch it, we see things through a broader lens. Expectations are exposed as meaningless—soul gifts come in unexpected packaging. Most everything significant that happens to us is revealed as grist for the soul mill, necessary learnings on the path home. The ladder to heaven is made from broken rungs.

Lite-dimmers: Individuals who have a tendency to undermine positive intentionality and good energy in others.

Material bypass: The tendency to get lodged in the material world (practical matters, earthly concerns) in an effort to avoid spiritual experience and uncomfortable emotions.

Nervous breakthrough: A profound (and courageous) emotional cleansing, a collapse of the false structures that have ruled our life, a breaking through to a more genuine state of consciousness. Often mischaracterized as a nervous breakdown. The key to the breakthrough is seeing the collapse all the way through to resolution.

The power of then: The effect the past has on our present consciousness. Although the physical body travels forward chronologically, one's emotional consciousness always lingers at any point of departure. To move forward on the path, we have to go back and deal with the wounds and memories that obstruct us. We've got to *be there then* before we can *be here now*.

The presumption of Essence: The tendency to see Essence everywhere we look, particularly in others. We look beyond the armor and recognize the beautiful being that is living below.

Sacred grumbles: Frustrations that emanate from the soul itself, indications that the soul wants to ascend to the next stage of its evolution. These frustrations can be humanifest in many forms, not always readily obvious.

The School of Heart Knocks: Life.

Selective attachment: In the context of soulshaping, selective attachment is the process of sifting everything through an essential filter, connecting only to those experiences and relationships that support true-path. We endeavor to make soul-serving choices at every turn. If something supports our ascension, we bring it on. If it doesn't, we stay away.

Self-distractive behavior: Any behavior done with the intention of avoiding our true self and authentic felt experience.

Shtuscle: Inner muscle, the soul-driven determination to deal with whatever obstacles come our way in our efforts to excavate and actualize our innate image for this lifetime. A term embodied by my grandparents, who endured all manner of struggle and still managed to keep their hearts (and their kitchen) open.

Soul-scriptures: The transcript of the innate image, the form that our lessons, experiences, and callings take.

Soul-shadows: Reminders of our calling(s) cast by our soul throughout our lives. These beacons of light shadow us wherever we go, always calling us home.

Soul-traces: Images of individual or collective soul history that enter our consciousness.

Soulitude: Undistracted time alone with your soul-self.

Soulpod: That person or group of people whom our soul finds the most resonance with at any given moment. It can include anyone that appears on our path to inform and catalyze our expansion—our biological family, significant figures, strangers with a lesson. People of soulnificance.

Soulshaping: The idea that our soul comes into each lifetime in a particular form, with a natural inclination to evolve beyond it. Our innate image represents the next shape in its evolution. It is the form we are here to embody and humanifest, the next step in our movement toward wholeness.

Soul sheen: A glow that emanates from us when we are living from the heart of true-path. Bright eyed, bushy-tailed, golden hue....

(The) Soulular phone: Your pipeline to divinity, the soulular phone connects your individual path to Universal Consciousness. When it rings, be sure to answer it. It is the divine Mother calling to remind you of the next step on your journey. The more inner work you have done to clear the lines, the clearer the connection.

Spiritual bypass: The tendency to jump to spirit prematurely, usually in an effort to avoid various aspects of earthly reality. The opposite of *Ascending with both feet on the ground.*

Spiritual emergingcy: The state of confusion and inner tumult that one experiences when a spiritual path/awareness is forcing its way into consciousness, prior to its full emergence and integration. See also spiritual emergency, elaborated on in depth by Stanislav and Christina Grof.

Survivalism: A state of being that is oriented around our survival and the satisfaction of our basic needs. Often an anxiety-driven way of being. To be distinguished from an Essence-centered way of being.

Survivalist guilt: The guilt we may experience when we shift from survivalism as our primary orientation toward a more subtle and essential way of being.

True-path: Any path that is true to our entelechy in this lifetime. The paths we are here to wander.

Truth ache: A form of sacred grumble, a truth ache is a nudging sense of falsity, a palpable hunger for true-path. Although sometimes painful, and although embracing it may well force us to turn our habitual patterns upside down in order to effect change, it contains the seeds of our transformation. When we repress it, truth decay sets in, and the only thing that can save us is a truth canal. Sometimes we wait too long, and we lose our truth altogether.

The Universal Broadcasting System (UBS): The dynamic and benevolent network of relatedness that brings lessons and messengers onto our path in an effort to grow our soul to the next level of consciousness. Serendipity Central. The universe presents us with endless opportunities to synchronize our path with our truth.

Selected Bibliography

Achterberg, Jeanne, and Rothberg, D. (1996). "Relationship as spiritual practice." *ReVision* 19 (Fall): 2–7.

Achterberg, Jeanne (1998). "Uncommon Bonds: On the spiritual nature of relationships." *ReVision* 21(2): 4–10.

Barks, Coleman (tr.). *Birdsong: 53 Short Poems.* Atlanta: Maypop, 1993.

Barks, Coleman (tr.). *The Essential Rumi.* San Francisco: HarperCollins, 1995.

Barks, Coleman (tr). *The Illuminated Rumi.* New York: Broadway, 1997.

Barks, Coleman, and Moyne, John (tr). *Unseen Rain.* Boston: Shambhala, 1986.

Gafni, Marc. *Soul Prints: Your Path to Fulfillment.* New York: Atria, 2002.

Green, Michael (tr.). *One Song: A New Illuminated Rumi.* Ithaca, NY: Perseus, 2005.

Grof, Christina, and Grof, Stanislav. *The Stormy Search for the Self.* New York: Tarcher/Putnam, 1990.

Harvey, Andrew (tr.). *Love's Glory: Re-Creations of Rumi.* Berkeley, CA: North Atlantic Books, 1996.

Hillman, James. *The Soul's Code: In Search of Character and Calling.* New York: Warner Books, 1996.

Hoffman, Edward. *The Right to be Human: A Biography of Abraham Maslow.* Los Angeles, CA: Tarcher, 1988.

Hopkins, Jeffrey (ed. and tr.). *The Dalai Lama at Harvard.* Ithaca, NY: Snow Lion, 1989.

Houston, Jean. *A Mythic Life.* San Francisco: HarperCollins, 1996.

Houston, Jean. *The Search for the Beloved.* New York: Tarcher/Penguin, 1987.

Judith, Anodea. *Eastern Body, Western Mind.* Berkeley, CA: Celestial Arts, 1996.

Keller, Helen. *The Open Door.* New York: Doubleday, 1957.

Lowen, Alexander. *Bioenergetics.* New York: Penguin, 1976.

Lowen, Alexander. *Joy.* New York: Penguin Arkana, 1995.

Maslow, Abraham. *Motivation and Personality* (2nd ed.). New York: Harper & Row, 1970.

Maslow, Abraham. *The Farther Reaches of Human Nature*. New York: Viking Press, 1971.

Maslow, Abraham. *Toward a Psychology of Being* (2nd ed.). Toronto: D. Van Nostrand Co., 1968.

Masters, Robert Augustus. *Divine Dynamite* (Revised Edition). USA: Tehmenos Press, 2006.

Oliver, Mary. *Dream Work*. New York: Atlantic Monthly Press, 1986.

Plato. *The Republic* (translated by Benjamin Jowett). Found online thanks to The Gutenberg Project.

Ram Dass. *Still Here*. New York: Riverhead Books, 2000.

Star, Jonathan (tr.). *In the Arms of the Beloved*. New York: Tarcher Putnam, 1997.

Trungpa, Chögyam. *Cutting Through Spiritual Materialism*. Boston: Shambhala, 1973.

Permissions

The publishers have generously given permission to use quotations from the following copyrighted works.

From *Unseen Rain: Quatrains of Rumi,* translated by John Moyne and Coleman Barks. Copyright ©1986 by Coleman Barks. Reprinted by arrangement with Shambhala Publications Inc., Boston, MA. www.shambhala.com.

From *The Search for the Beloved,* by Jean Houston. Copyright ©1986 by Jean Houston. Used by permission of Jeremy P. Tarcher, an imprint of Penguin Group (USA) Inc.

From *A Mythic Life,* by Jean Houston. Copyright© 1996 by Jean Houston. Used by permission of Harper Collins Publishers, San Francisco.

From *The Essential Rumi,* translated by Coleman Barks. Copyright © 1995 by Coleman Barks. Permission granted by Coleman Barks, Harper Collins, San Francisco.

From *Dreamwork,* by Mary Oliver. Copyright © 1986 by Mary Oliver. Used by permission of Grove/Atlantic Inc.

From *Soul Prints: Path to Fulfillments,* by Marc Gafni. Copyright © 2001 by Mark Gafni. Reprinted by permission of Atria Books, a division of Simon & Schuster, Inc.

From *Anaïs Nin.* Permission granted by The Anaïs Nin Trust in arrangement with Barbara W. Stuhlmann, author's representative.

From *The Illuminated Rumi,* translated by Coleman Barks, illuminations by Michael Green. Copyright ©1997 by Coleman Barks and Michael Green. Used by permission of Broadway Books, a division of Random House, Inc.

From *Cutting Through Spiritual Materialism,* by Chögyam Trungpa. Copyright © 1973 by Chögyam Trungpa. Reprinted by arrangement with Shambhala Publications Inc., Boston, MA. www.shambhala.com.

From *Eastern Body, Western Mind,* by Anodea Judith. Copyright © 1996. Reprinted by permission of Celestial Arts (Ten-Speed Press), Berkeley, CA.

From *Rumi Birdsong: 53 Short Poems*, translated by Coleman Barks. Copyright © 1993 by Coleman Barks. Reprinted by permission of MayPop Books.

From *The Open Door*, by Helen Keller. Copyright © 1957 by Helen Keller. Used by permission of Doubleday, a division of Random House, Inc.

From *Love's Glory: Re-Creations of Rumi*, by Andrew Harvey, published by North Atlantic Books. Copyright © 1996 by Andrew Harvey. Reprinted by permission of publisher.

From *Rumi: In the Arms of the Beloved* by Rumi, translated by Jonathan Star. Copyright © 1997 by Jonathan Star. Used by permission of Jeremy P. Tarcher, an imprint of Penguin Group (USA) Inc.

From *Divine Dynamite (Revised Edition)*, by Robert Augustus Masters. Copyright © 2006 by Robert Augustus Masters. Permission by Robert Augustus Masters.

From *The Dalai Lama of Harvard*, edited and translated by Jeffrey Hopkins. Copyright © 1989 by Jeffrey Hopkins. Used by permission of Snow Lion Publications.

From *One Song: A New Illuminated Rumi*, translated by Michael Green. Copyright © 2005 by Michael Green. Perseus, Ithaca, NY.

From *Joy*, by Alexander Lowen, PhD. Copyright © 1995 by Alexander Lowen. Used by permission of Viking Penguin, a division of Penguin Group (USA) Inc.

From *Still Here*, by Ram Dass. Copyright © 2000 by Ram Dass. River Head Books (Penguin).

Permission to use the term "material buy-pass" given by Dr. Jessica Weiser.

About the Author

Born in Toronto, Canada, JEFF BROWN did all the things he was supposed to do to become successful in the eyes of the world. He was on the Dean's Honor List as an undergraduate. He won the Law and Medicine prize in law school. He apprenticed with top criminal lawyer Eddie Greenspan. It had been Brown's lifelong dream to practice criminal law and search for the truth in the courtroom.

But then, on the verge of opening a law practice, he heard a little voice inside telling him to stop, just stop. With great difficulty, he honored this voice and began a heartfelt quest for the truth that lived within him. Although he didn't realize it at the time, Brown was actually questing for his innate image, the essential being that he came into this lifetime to embody. He was searching for his authentic face.

As part of his journey, Brown surrendered to his confusion and explored many possible paths. He studied Bioenergetics and did session work with cofounder Alexander Lowen. He practiced as a body-centered psychotherapist. He completed an MA in Psychology at Saybrook Graduate School in San Francisco and cofounded the Open Heart Gang, a benevolent gang with a heartfelt intention. He developed his student business and became a successful entrepreneur.

The most important thing Brown did, however, was the inner work. By going inside and connecting his spirituality with his emotional life, he learned essential lessons. By learning to surrender to the "School of Heart Knocks" (the school of life), he found his authentic face and embraced the call to write *Soulshaping*. Although he resisted it at first, he soon realized that honoring the call was his best defense against sleeplessness. If he wrote, he slept. If he didn't, he lay awake all night. This is the nature of a calling.

Brown currently lives in Toronto, where he and the Open Heart Gang are close to finishing a documentary about Bhagavan Das (of *Be Here Now* fame). The film, titled *Karmageddon*, includes wonderful dialogues with Brown and spiritual teacher Ram Dass, yogis Seane Corn and David Newman, and chanters Deva Premal and Miten. In addition, Brown is actively searching for wheels for the Soulshaping bus tour, a spirited adventure across North America with his soul-friends, heaven-bent on inviting more people to raise the flag of the little voice to the rafters of consciousness.